CONTENTS

AN INTRODUCTION TO THE SERIES

Such is the pace of historical enquiry in the modern world that there is an ever-widening gap between the specialist article or monograph, incorporating the results of current research, and general surveys, which inevitably become out of date. *Seminar Studies in History* are designed to bridge this gap. The series was founded by Patrick Richardson in 1966 and his aim was to cover major themes in British, European and World history. Between 1980 and 1996 Roger Lockyer continued his work, before handing the editorship over to Clive Emsley and Gordon Martel. Clive Emsley is Professor of History at the Open University, while Gordon Martel is Professor of International History at the University of Northern British Columbia, Canada and Senior Research Fellow at De Montfort University.

All the books are written by experts in their field who are not only familiar with the latest research but have often contributed to it. They are frequently revised, in order to take account of new information and interpretations. They provide a selection of documents to illustrate major themes and provoke discussion, and also a guide to further reading. The aim of *Seminar Studies* is to clarify complex issues without over-simplifying them, and to stimulate readers into deepening their knowledge and understanding of major themes and topics.

ACKNOWLEDGEMENTS

The publishers would like to thank Faber and Faber Ltd for permission to reproduce 'Markings' by Dag Hammerskjöld, translated by Leif Sjöberg and W. H. Auden, published in 1964.

NOTE ON REFERENCING SYSTEM

Readers should note that numbers in square brackets [5] refer them to the corresponding entry in the Bibliography at the end of the book (specific page numbers are given in italics). A number in square brackets preceded by Doc. [Doc. 5] refers readers to the corresponding item in the Documents section which follows the main text.

PREFACE

The peacekeeping function of the United Nations (UN) occupied a central position in the organization's role during the cold war from the late 1940s until the late 1980s. At various points during this period the UN appeared to provide merely an arena of conflict rather than, as intended, a forum for co-operation. At these times its peacekeeping and military observation ventures provided a sustaining strand of political worth at the core of the organization. Peacekeeping filled a part, however small and qualified, of the vacuum created by the paralysis inflicted on collective security by the polarization of the international system between east and west. It provided an 'immunization' against the infection of a global ideological contest, which might otherwise have spread uncontrolled into every local disorder. 'Voluntarism', moral pressure and physical interposition were, in theory if not always in practice, the 'weapons' of peacekeeping. Its purpose was to create conditions for finding solutions to conflicts rather than to provide these solutions. This stood in contrast to the enforcement of outcomes by joint military endeavour that underlay the concept of collective security. Inevitably, therefore, the applicability of the peacekeeping method was limited. There were limitations too in the areas of operation 'permitted' to it by the superpowers themselves. Peacekeeping was in essence a 'peripheral' remedy, barred from a role in areas of core interest to the superpowers. While the Middle East was consistently the object of the peacekeepers' attentions, they had no contribution to make during the cold war in Europe or in Southeast Asia. But it was in this very modesty of methods, aims and scope that the strength of peacekeeping lay. 'Aggressive' peacekeeping – whether in political or military terms – would have been a self-contradiction. Its continuation was always dependant on the favour – or at least acquiescence – of the permanent members of the Security Council, who set their own acceptable limits for it.

The purpose of this *Seminar Study* is to locate the peacekeeping phenomenon within the broader history of the cold war and particularly of the United Nations as a key institution of the time. In pursuit of this, the parallel histories of superpower relations and of peacekeeping are explored and particular attention is given to the processes by which changes in the former determined the character of the latter. To provide the broadest possible context for this, the analysis is also concerned with pre-cold war thinking on multilateral intervention and, more substantially, the impact of the end of the cold war on UN peacekeeping. The end of the cold war changed fundamentally the political environment in which the United Nations operated. Initially, the 'liberation' from bipolarity was seen by many as a new dawn for peacekeeping – even, perhaps, an opportunity for the reinvigoration of full-scale collective security. In general, this optimism does not seem to have been justified. The removal of the cold war dimension has brought, perhaps, as many new problems for UN peacekeeping as it has solved old ones. Nevertheless, peacekeeping operations mushroomed in both number and ambition in the decade after the end of the cold war. It seems certain that the fundamental aims and methods of peacekeeping will continue to characterize multilateral interventions in local conflicts, whether by the UN itself, regional bodies or combinations of the two. It is, in this respect, a valuable legacy of an otherwise dark period in twentieth-century international history.

For B & C

ABBREVIATIONS AND ACRONYMS

ANC	Congolese National Army
CIA	Central Intelligence Agency (US)
CIS	Commonwealth of Independent States (former Soviet Union)
ECOWAS	Economic Community of West African States
I–FOR	Implementation Force (Bosnia)
ICJ	International Court of Justice
MFO	Multinational Force and Observers (Sinai)
MINURSO	United Nations Mission for the Referendum in Western Sahara
MNF (I–II)	Multinational Force (Lebanon)
MONUA	United Nations Observation Mission in Angola
MSC	Military Staff Committee (Security Council)
NATO	North Atlantic Treaty Organization
ONUC	United Nations Operation in Congo
ONUCA	United Nations Observer Group in Central America
ONUMOZ	United Nations Operation in Mozambique
ONUSAL	United Nations Observation Mission in El Salvador
OSCE	Organization for Security and Co-operation in Europe
PLO	Palestine Liberation Organization
UAR	United Arab Republic
UNAMIR	United Nations Assistance Mission for Rwanda
UNAVEM (I–III)	United Nations Angola Verification Mission
UNDOF	United Nations Disengagement Observation Force (Golan Heights)
UNEF (I–II)	United Nations Emergency Force (Suez–Sinai)
UNFICYP	United Nations Force in Cyprus

UNGOMAP	United Nations Good Offices Mission in Afghanistan and Pakistan
UNIFIL	United Nations Interim Force in Lebanon
UNIIMOG	United Nations Iran–Iraq Military Observer Group
UNIKOM	United Nations Iraq–Kuwait Observation Mission
UNIPOM	United Nations India–Pakistan Observation Mission
UNITAF	Unified Task Force (Somalia)
UNMIH	United Nations Mission in Haiti
UNMOGIP	United Nations Military Observer Group in India and Pakistan
UNMOT	United Nations Mission of Observers in Tajikistan
UNOGIL	United Nations Observation Group in Lebanon
UNOMIG	United Nations Observer Mission in Georgia
UNOMIL	United Nations Observer Mission in Liberia
UNOMUR	United Nations Observer Mission Uganda–Rwanda
UNOSOM (I–II)	United Nations Operation in Somalia
UNPROFOR	United Nations Protection Force (former Yugoslavia)
UNSF	United Nations Security Force (West New Guinea)
UNTAC	United Nations Transitional Authority in Cambodia
UNTAG	United Nations Transition Assistance Group (Namibia)
UNTEA	United Nations Temporary Executive Authority (West New Guinea)
UNTSO	United Nations Truce Supervision Organization (Middle East)
UNYOM	United Nations Yemen Observeration Mission

PART ONE: THE BACKGROUND

1 BEGINNINGS: THE ESTABLISHMENT OF THE UNITED NATIONS AND ITS SECURITY FUNCTIONS

THE LEGACY OF THE LEAGUE

Comparisons between the League of Nations and the United Nations usually emphasize the contrasts between the two organizations rather than their similarities. This was an understandable tendency at the foundation of the UN and in its early development. The League, after all, had failed to prevent the Second World War, in the aftermath of which the new organization was being forged. In order to 'sell' the United Nations to potentially sceptical national politicians and publics, its advocates had to claim a uniqueness for it which distanced it from a discredited predecessor. In reality, however, the League of Nations provided the blueprint for the new organization in terms of both its organization and its basic objectives. The profoundly innovative character of the League of Nations in the context of the post-First World War international system is generally overlooked. Its structure – an 'executive' Council of the big powers and a 'parliamentary' Assembly of all state members, both managed by an international 'civil service' – represented a bold transposition of domestic constitutional arrangements to the international environment. Like many bold ideas, of course, this approach has been seen in hindsight as more obvious than it was in its own historical setting. The fundamental 'logic' of the League's structure meant that any successor organization would naturally tend to adopt the same basic architecture. Similarly, the *purposes* of the League, or at any rate those envisioned by its American planners and their supporters, were also startlingly revolutionary. Responsibility for national defence and security was, as far as possible, to be removed from the sovereign state. The fears and insecurities that had hitherto generated the arms races and aggressive alliances apparently at the root of the catastrophe of 1914–18 would be alleviated by the construction of nothing less than a 'new world order'. It was now proposed that the security of individual states would be the collective responsibility of the world community working through the structures of its new League. Again, this new 'multi-lateralism' was both strikingly bold and somehow obvious, and the basic idea outlived the League itself.

In many respects during its first decade the League made a valuable contribution to the management of the post-war international system. Throughout the 1920s it provided mediation in border disputes at various times between Finland and Sweden, Yugoslavia and Albania, and Hungary and Czechoslovakia. The League also brought a new moral sensibility to colonialism when, instead of the colonies of the defeated powers in 1918 simply being transferred to the victors, they were made the responsibility of the League, which 'mandated' their administration and responsibility for their eventual self-determination to 'appropriate' member states. It had also initiated what could later be seen as prototype international peacekeeping operations. One such force was deployed in the disputed Saar territory between France and Germany. In the aftermath of the war the Saar was removed from German sovereignty and 'internationalized' pending an act of self-determination in 1935. An international administration and security force also controlled Danzig (the modern day Polish city of Gdansk), which was removed from German administration and declared a Free City until it was forcibly reintegrated into Germany by the Nazis in 1939.

The failure of the US Congress to ratify American membership of the League despite the leading role of President Woodrow Wilson in its creation as part of the Versailles peace treaty was, of course, a fatal drawback in the longer term. The passing of the organization's leadership to the diplomatically more traditional Europeans like Britain and France inevitably affected its basic character. Additionally, the nature of international relations in the 1920s contrasted sharply with that of the following decade. By the early 1930s the international environment had begun to change. The 'post-traumatic' calm of the immediate post-war years gave way to a new instability. Territorial and ideological revisionism on the part of states that for various reasons rejected the post-Versailles *status quo* threw down the gauntlet to the League, whose origins were inextricably tied to that settlement. And, it must be said, the League itself bore some responsibility for this hostility. Not only had it been born of the Versailles treaty but in its first years it had excluded from membership a number of key powers, most notably Germany and the Soviet Union. Their eventual admission could not eradicate their sense of exclusion from the system which the League sought to manage.

In this deteriorating climate the capacity of the League to translate collective security from theory into a practical tool of international relations was now tested. The collective security procedures of the League were outlined in Article 10 of its basic constitution, the Covenant [Doc. 1]. Collective measures were to be undertaken to preserve the territorial integrity of member states 'against external aggression'. Tellingly, however, the means by which this was to be done were left vague. The League Council had the responsibility to advise on methods to be employed when necessary. The strongest instrument of enforcement that members were supposedly required to apply on the 'direction' of the Council was economic sanctions. The Council might 'recommend' military action but members were under no obligation to comply (Article 16) [65 p. 17]. On the rare occasions when economic sanctions were implemented, many members simply declined to participate in them.

In this way Italy's aggression against the African state of Abyssinia (Ethiopia) in 1935 effectively went unpunished when a belatedly applied raft of sanctions was disregarded by states that for political or economic reasons did not wish to confront the Fascist regime in Rome [66 pp. 32–6]. Even this débâcle seemed a robust response in comparison to the League's failure to initiate any collective security measures against Japan after its invasion of Manchuria in northern China in 1931. In both cases the central weakness in the concept of collective security in a world of sovereign states was exposed. However highminded and idealistic the original conception of the League advanced by Woodrow Wilson and his supporters, older and harder realities governed the behaviour of the states that now dominated the institution. States like Britain and France had traditionally conducted their foreign policies on the basis of narrowly defined national interests. The calculation of these interests rarely went beyond considerations of the physical security of the state and its economic well-being [72 pp. 134–5]. The more generous conception of national interest as being best safeguarded by a just and secure global system – the conception at the heart of collective security thinking – did not progress during the life of the League. In a sense a vacuum of ideas had been created by the withdrawal of Wilson's powerful moral advocacy. The League retreated, amidst a newly dangerous set of international circumstances, from the ethical high ground it originally sought to occupy. The fate of China at the hands of Japan featured hardly at all when the powers which made up the League Council made their respective calculations of national interests. Italy, being closer to the centre of a still predominantly European international system, was more problematic – but not much more. In the latter half of the 1930s, as the world stumbled towards another general war, the League became wholly marginalized in the dynamics of international relations. National security remained, as it always had been, the responsibility of the individual state and such others with which it could form alliances. Once more the cycle of inter-state conflict, system breakdown and resolution by generalized war would precede a new attempt to reconstruct international security on a multilateral basis. As we have noted, though, the new project did not begin from a *tabula rasa*. The model and the experience of the League were there to be drawn upon [87; 97].

CONTENDING VISIONS, EARLY CONFLICTS

The concept of the United Nations developed by stages after the entry of the United States into the war in December 1941. In August of that year (four months before Pearl Harbor), at a ship-board meeting between the US president Franklin Roosevelt and British prime minister Winston Churchill, the notion of collective security for a future post-war world was resurrected. The Atlantic Charter which emerged from this meeting expressed the view that 'all nations of the world, for realistic as well as spiritual reasons, must come to the abandonment of the use of force' and spoke of 'the establishment of a ... permanent system of general security' [*Doc. 2*]. By the beginning of 1942, with the United States now in the war, the twenty-six anti-Axis powers affirmed their commitment to this declaration and, for the first time, styled themselves the 'United Nations'. During the remaining years of the war ideas for the new peacetime organization developed. They did so, of course, under considerable constraints. The overriding priority for the Allied states was the war itself. Extensive speculation on the nature of the post-war international system would have been a misuse of political energies. Additionally, Roosevelt, who like President Wilson a quarter of a century earlier, was at the forefront of thinking about the new institution, was anxious to avoid a repeat of the isolationist backlash that had prevented American participation in the League. Roosevelt's initial ideas centred on the management of security by the big powers, primarily the United States, Britain, the Soviet Union and, perhaps, China [76 *p. 56*]. The exercise of this responsibility would, in his view, be made possible by the generalized disarmament of the other powers of the international system. Churchill, from a more sceptical European perspective, was less confident that the necessary co-operation could be achieved among the big powers for such a plan to be feasible. In his view, states would continue to define their national interests in the same narrow way that had undermined the League's attempts to implement collective security. The participation of the United States in the new order would be a positive advance, but it would be unlikely to alter the basic character of national foreign policies. The British prime minister was also concerned at the marginalization of the smaller and middle-sized powers implicit in Roosevelt's proposed security regime. This worry was connected with Churchill's evolving view that a strong European dimension should be central to post-war Britain's external relations. He therefore favoured a new organization with a distinct regional rather than global structure. The new body should, ideally, be one in which loose world-wide arrangements acted as an umbrella for strong local inter-governmental institutions [83 *pp. 19–21*].

At the Tehran conference in November 1943, when the tide of the war was clearly turning in the Allies' favour, the Soviet Union was brought into the debate. Stalin was now briefed on the American idea of the 'four policemen' (the major Allied powers) as a global 'executive' deploying military enforcement powers at the head of a world assembly. The Soviet leader, like Churchill, was wary of the concentration of power in so few hands and initially shared the British preference for a strong regional dimension to any new security regime. However, Roosevelt warned Stalin that American public opinion, still influenced by isolationist thinking, might not accept US involvement in security commitments determined by local states in other parts of the world. In view of this Stalin moved towards the more centralized conception of the Americans [83 *p. 24*]. As with the League, it was the Americans who seized the initiative on the construction of the new organization and who worked their conception around the doubts of the other key actors. On both occasions this was no more than a reflection of the balance of power among the respective sets of Allies – an ironic situation, perhaps, as the collective security project was designed exactly to remove considerations of national power from international security.

It was a largely American plan which was put forward for discussion when Allied representatives met to confirm the outlines of the new organization in August 1944. The sequence of meetings in which this took place was held at Dumbarton Oaks, a country house near Washington. The key negotiators here were the Soviet and British ambassadors to the United States, Andrei Gromyko and Sir Alexander

Cadogan, and the American assistant secretary of state, Edward Stettinius, who acted as chairman. Nationalist China was also represented, but not in the central negotiations. The intention was to reach a consensus among the four powers and then to present the wider anti-Axis alliance with an agreed blueprint. Agreement was quickly reached on the basic institutional form of the new United Nations. This was clearly influenced by the example of the League. There would be a Security Council of eleven members (later increased to fifteen). This would consist of the five big anti-Axis powers: the United States, the Soviet Union, Britain, China and France (now admitted as a 'fifth policeman'). These would be the 'permanent members' and each would have the power of veto over Council decisions. In addition six (later ten) non-permanent members – without power of veto – would be appointed on a rolling basis from the various regions represented in the organization. All member states would have a seat in a General Assembly. Both the Security Council and the General Assembly would be serviced by a secretariat of international civil servants headed by a secretary-general. A nascent system of collective security was also approved at Dumbarton Oaks. Disputes between members would in the first instance be settled by processes of negotiation, mediation and conciliation among the protagonists. If these failed the problem would become the responsibility of the Security Council, which would propose its own settlement terms. If this also failed then the Council could apply economic and other sanctions against the 'aggressor' with, in the last resort, recourse to military action. All members of the United Nations would be required to commit themselves legally to undertake such action on the instructions of the Security Council. The Council would itself be advised on the strategic and operational aspects of these measures by a Military Staff Committee made up of senior military representatives of its permanent members [90; 100].

Despite those wide areas of agreement, significant points remained at issue after Dumbarton Oaks. Some of these were essentially technical. There was dispute over the extent of the commitments to be required of UN members and the nature of preparedness and ear-marking of national forces for UN service. More ominously, though, a profoundly important issue remained unresolved at Dumbarton Oaks: the voting system in both General Assembly and Security Council, which, by extension, touched on the question of national representation.

In the case of the General Assembly the Soviet Union sought representation for all sixteen of its constituent republics. This would obviously have been a misuse of the concept of 'sovereign equality' on which the UN was to be based – the principle that all independent states in the international system should have equal rights and powers. But the Soviet position was in some ways understandable. Although the world had yet to fall into the extremes of cold war bipolarity between capitalist west and communist east, the rudiments of this global cleavage had been present virtually since the Bolshevik revolution of 1917. It did not take any great prescience on the part of Stalin and his representatives at Dumbarton Oaks to see east–west divisions as a major feature of the new organization in the future. The Soviet Union was at this time clearly disadvantaged in terms of simple arithmetic since Dumbarton Oaks was held before the creation of the 'people's democracies' of eastern Europe and therefore of a communist 'bloc'. It would be ideologically isolated in the new organization. The idea of sovereign equality had a certain moral force in an international system whose states were personified as strong and weak individuals; in a world based on collectively secured 'justice' the rights of the weak should obviously be as great as those of the strong. But the international system was in reality composed of hugely divergent populations and territories. In this real world sovereign equality was inequitable. Why should El Salvador, for example (another founder member), have the same powers in the global polity as the incomparably larger and more populous Soviet Union?

The conflict over the Security Council related to the veto power of the five permanent members. There was no disagreement on the basic principle. The delegates at Dumbarton Oaks all agreed that it was a necessary mechanism. It was in fact an advance on the voting system operated at the League where, in Assembly as well as Council, unanimity was required before any action could be taken. The proposed UN veto was for the permanent members of the Security Council alone and would only be activated by a negative vote, not merely by abstention or absence. The difficulty that emerged at Dumbarton Oaks was over restrictions on its use. The British and Americans argued that the veto should not be available to a permanent member when its own behaviour was the subject of discussion. Once again aware of its political vulnerability in an overwhelmingly western institution, the Soviet Union insisted that the veto should be an absolute right of the great powers in all Security Council business.

Agreement on both these issues eluded the ambassadors over the six weeks of the Dumbarton Oaks talks. Subsequent attempts to settle them in the remaining months of 1944 were also unsuccessful. The search for an agreement now passed up to the Allied foreign ministers – rather than their ambassadors in Washington – when they met at

Yalta in February 1945. Molotov for the Soviet Union gave some ground by accepting a restriction on the veto where 'peaceful settlement' rather than collective security 'enforcement' in issues affecting permanent members was under discussion. With rather more difficulty a compromise was also reached on the issue of General Assembly representation. It was accepted that the Soviet Union could have two further seats for the republics of Ukraine and Byelorussia. Roosevelt agreed to this only reluctantly, having at one point threatened to demand separate representation for all of the then forty-eight states of the United States if Stalin did not give way [100 *p. 27*]. These relatively small western concessions, though, were seen as a reasonable price for progress towards the inauguration of the new organization.

This took place formally in San Francisco at the end of April 1945. It followed an invitation from the five permanent members of the proposed Security Council to fifty states who were then anti-Axis belligerents. This was a status acquired only very recently by some states as the outcome of the war had become plain and the prizes that went with being on the winning side beckoned. The result was a swelling of the ranks of founding members, which bolstered the new organization's commitment to the ideal of universality of membership. The absence of such universality, it will be recalled, had been a major defect of the League system. Franklin Roosevelt had died ten days before the opening of the San Francisco session, but his successor, Harry Truman, immediately affirmed his – and America's – commitment to the new organization. This was greeted with relief among many who had feared a recurrence of the isolationism that ended American participation at a similar stage in the development of the League. In reality, however, the prevailing trend in American politics in 1944 and 1945 was anti-isolationist, and Roosevelt's Democratic administration had already sought to ensure a bipartisan approach to the new United Nations. Stettinius, elevated to secretary of state after the November 1944 presidential election, co-operated closely with the Republican's principal foreign affairs adviser (and future secretary of state), John Foster Dulles, who accepted an invitation to participate in the San Francisco conference [31 *pp. 163–4*].

Driven on by the 'big five', whose authority was enhanced by their leadership of a huge military alliance poised on the verge of final victory, the San Francisco conference ratified the decisions taken at Dumbarton Oaks and Yalta. The structure of the institution, familiar in outline to most of the participants from their League experience, was accepted without demur. Similarly, the basic constitution of the United Nations, its Charter, which was essentially an American-composed document, was adopted with only marginal and technical modifications. At the centre of the Charter – and of the world organization's ambition – was a new and supposedly comprehensive system of global security. It appeared from this that the lesson taken from the League was not that collective security was an unattainable ideal in a world of sovereign states, but rather that with the right legal and political structures it could be made to work [83; 90].

THE CHARTER AND COLLECTIVE SECURITY

The legal-constitutional basis of the UN's collective security ambitions was to be found in Chapter VII of the Charter, which was concerned with 'Action with Respect to Threats to the Peace, Breaches of the Peace, and Acts of Aggression' [*Doc. 3(i)*]. The scheme laid out here was essentially that which had been agreed at Dumbarton Oaks and which has already been briefly described. The first of the twelve Articles of Chapter VII, Article 39, gave the Security Council the responsibility of determining when a situation required collective security action and what form that action should take. It thus underlined from the outset the predominance of the Security Council in the process. The following three articles provided an escalating series of measures available to the Council in enforcing its collective will. Article 40 dealt with 'provisional measures' that the Council might insist on prior to determining enforcement action. The nature of such provisional measures was not elucidated in the Charter, but they were generally assumed to include demands for cease-fires and troop withdrawals. Article 41 dealt with substantive but non-military enforcement action of the type that had been tried unsuccessfully by the League. These were explicitly identified as economic sanctions, transport and communications boycotts and the interruption of diplomatic relations, though other steps might also be taken as long as they fell short of military action. The military options were dealt with in Article 42, which empowered the Security Council to take such action as necessary 'to restore international peace and security' using the 'air, sea or land forces of Members of the United Nations'. It is at this point that the similarities between the respective collective security concepts of the League and the United Nations disappear. The divergence became even more obvious in Article 43. This outlined the nature and extent of members' commitments and made not only co-operation with, but participation in, military measures obligatory for all Charter signatories if the Security Council should require it. On the call of the Security Council, members would be required to provide forces and facilities to enforce UN decisions against aggressor states. These forces were to be provided under the terms of prior agreements, but these would be essentially technical and could not be a means of evading participation.

The arrangements envisaged under Article 43, if they had ever been properly implemented, would have been just one step short of the creation of a UN standing army. The idea of a permanent international force had been discussed in the past; it had at one stage been proposed for the League. But there was general agreement among the big powers in 1944 and 1945 that such an arrangement would raise too many practical and political difficulties. Issues of financing, training and equipment as well as larger questions over national sovereignty would probably have been insurmountable. Under Article 43 most of the advantages of a permanent force would have been gained with none of these disadvantages. The details of the Military Staff Committee (MSC) which was to direct the enforcement of collective security (and which had first been suggested at Dumbarton Oaks) were contained in Article 47. The MSC was to be composed of the chiefs of staff of the five permanent members. It was to advise the Council on military enforcement operations and undertake their strategic direction. The MSC, at the apex of the collective security machinery, quickly became redundant as the cold war set in and the relationship between the chiefs of staff of the bipolar blocs became anything but co-operative.

The final part of Chapter VII, Article 51, was the only one which suggested any significant limitation on the power of the Security Council. It affirmed the 'inherent right of individual or collective self-defence'. The use of the term 'inherent' was significant in that it implied a natural order in which in the last resort states must have recourse to their own resources for their own defence. Regardless of the ambitions of the new organization in extending collective security, it stopped short of insisting on its *replacing* individual (or intra-alliance) security. Certain limits on Security Council 'absolutism' were implied too in Chapter VIII of the Charter, which also touched on collective security. Articles 52–54 dealt with 'Regional Arrangements' [*Doc. 3(ii)*]. Here some residual acknowledgement was given to the early position of Winston Churchill, which, it will be recalled, favoured a more decentralized collective security system. The legitimacy of 'regional arrangements' (in other words regional intergovernmental organizations) was recognized by Article 52, which acknowledged their potential role in the maintenance of security. Article 53, however, made it clear that such a role was ultimately dependent on the Security Council [*79 pp. 354–5*]. It was the Council which would 'where appropriate, utilize such regional arrangements or agencies for enforcement action *under its authority*' (emphasis added). Lip-service having been paid to local alliances and organizations, the over-arching authority of the Security Council was thus reasserted. The regional dimension to the security functions of the UN would be little considered during the cold war. Later, though, the issue would be revived as post-cold war peacekeeping demands threatened to outstrip the supply available from the centre and as increasingly assertive regional organizations sought legitimacy from the UN for their own actions [83; 90; 91].

The central importance given to the permanent members of the Security Council to the exclusion of other parts of the organization, which is evident in Chapters VII and VIII of the Charter, harks back to Roosevelt's wartime conception of the big powers as 'policemen'. Although somewhat adapted at Dumbarton Oaks, the basic purpose behind Roosevelt's thinking was clearly present in the final Charter. The intention here was to prevent the general institutional paralysis that had resulted from the diffusion of authority in the League. In the UN the Security Council alone would decide whether a situation warranted action. It, and it alone, would then determine the measures necessary to deal with the situation up to and including the use of force. Any such force would be directed by the military commanders of the permanent members. If regional organizations were to have a role it would be one initiated and closely supervised by the Security Council. While the United States saw the primacy of the Security Council as a precondition for the successful application of collective security, the Soviet Union supported it for different reasons. Conscious as always of its potential weakness in a forum based on the equality of sovereign representation, Moscow sought to retain the most important powers of the organization within the ambit of the veto [*Doc. 4*]. This coincidence of position on the part of the two emerging superpowers did not, however, prevent the eventual revelation of collective security as incompatible with the basic structure of international relations in a bipolar system.

Needless to say, the dominance of the Security Council, while acceptable to its permanent members, was not welcomed by all in the new organization. At San Francisco, Australia and New Zealand sought a larger role for the General Assembly in security matters than the Dumbarton Oaks plan had envisaged. A proposal by New Zealand that the Assembly should approve any enforcement action planned by the Council was quickly rejected. This would have threatened a repeat of the League's tendency to allow the decision-making process to run into the sands of generalized and inconclusive debate. The demands of the two Australasian states that the Assembly should have broad rights of discussion and the power to refer issues to the Security Council was, however, accepted and embodied in Articles 10 and 11 of the Charter [83 *p. 55*]. It was also agreed that the General Assembly should receive annual reports from the Security Council, a procedure which gave the impression if not the reality of democratic accountability. Beyond these limited concessions to the General Assembly, the Security Council also agreed to a special prerogative for the secretary-general. By the terms of Article 99 he could 'bring to the attention of the Security Council any matter which in his opinion may threaten the maintenance of international peace and security'. Although accepted as unexceptional by the big powers in 1945, this would have some significance to peacekeeping in the future [90].

Viewed from the glacial bipolarity into which the post-war international system quickly settled after 1945, the UN's emphasis on big power co-operation seemed wholly misplaced. How – it seemed reasonable to ask in the depths of the cold war – could there have been any hope of a viable collective security system emerging from a divided Security Council whose decisions were subject to veto by any one of its permanent members? In an ideologically riven international system virtually all international crises would be seen through the opposing lenses of bipolarity. There could be no objective evaluation of disputes let alone agreement on the identity of aggressors (and nowhere in the Charter was 'aggression' defined). Without such agreement there could be no enforcement and without enforcement collective security was meaningless. In 1945, however, perceptions and predictions were determined by factors specific to the time. It could be argued that the rapid development of the east–west conflict after the end of the Second World War caused later observers to underestimate the continuing impetus for co-operation among the wartime allies. Having spent several hard years locked in a struggle with a common enemy, it was a quite reasonable assumption that the Allies would maintain a unified sense of purpose in the post-war period. This must certainly have played a part in Roosevelt's early ideas of international security based on the disarmament of all but a small group of heavily armed 'policemen'. Previous conflicts, after all, had produced effective post-war regulatory mechanisms among allies with little in common in their domestic politics. The European 'concert' system following the end of the Napoleonic Wars in 1815 was an example of this. More immediately, but for the withdrawal of the United States the League might have proved a reasonably effective system of international security, founded though it was on the continuation of a wartime alliance. It must be borne in mind too that the technical-strategic circumstances which came to characterize the cold war – the mutual possession by the opposing blocks of thermonuclear weapons – did not exist while the Charter was being drafted. The bombing of Hiroshima and Nagasaki came four months after the San Francisco conference (and a full year after Dumbarton Oaks). The Soviet Union did not acquire any atomic weapons until 1949 and it was 1955 before both superpowers began their deterrent relationship based on roughly balanced nuclear capacities. While east–west tensions might be seen on the horizon, there was no reason to suppose that all international disputes would tend to merge into one conflict built around the unique military capability of the two superpowers.

These assumptions on the part of the big powers about their continuing co-operation should not, anyway, be over-stated. The immediate concern of the non-Soviet Allies during 1944 and 1945 was the war against Japan. Although the advanced planning for the United Nations took place in the triumphalism surrounding inevitable victory in Europe, the situation in Asia was much less settled. The United States was anxious to induce the Soviet Union (in this still pre-atomic phase) to commit its forces in Asia [76 *p. 61*]. Too much public exploration of future US–USSR conflicts would not have helped in this. The reality of wartime unity rather than assessments of post-war developments was still uppermost in the calculations of the White House and state department. Another perspective on the UN's original collective security mechanisms would not focus at all on assumptions of continuing unity but would, in a sense, take an opposite position. The concentration of authority in the Council and the power of veto could be seen as an acknowledgement of likely big power *division* and not unity. The location of any significant security powers in the General Assembly, where the Soviet Union would automatically be out-voted, would merely ensure Moscow's departure from the whole system. Likewise, safeguarding the national interests of the five permanent members through the power of veto, far from weakening collective security, was the minimum price to be paid for even the slimmest chance of its ever being implemented.

PART TWO: DESCRIPTIVE ANALYSIS

2 THE EMERGENCE OF PEACEKEEPING, 1948–1956

KOREA AND THE LIMITS OF COLLECTIVE SECURITY

The flaws inherent in the UN's collective security architecture could not remain unexposed as the cold war deepened. In some early crises in east–west relations, like that over Berlin in 1947–48, the UN had only a marginal role [83 pp. 218–21]. The position of the organization in the deteriorating conditions of the international system in the late 1940s was a difficult one. As international relations came to be determined by bipolar loyalties, the idea of a truly disinterested global body seemed more and more untenable. Assured of the support of the large majority of the membership, the United States came increasingly to regard the UN as an arm of its foreign policy. 'The United Nations', wrote one of Truman's aides in 1948, 'is a God-given vehicle through which the United States can build up a community of powers ... to resist Soviet aggression and maintain our historic interests' [66 p. 59]. In such a climate a reckoning for the new system could not be long delayed. It came in 1950 in Korea.

The western Allies had committed themselves early in the Second World War to securing the independence of Korea, which had been annexed by Japan in 1910. At the end of hostilities the northern part of Korea had been occupied by Soviet troops (after Moscow's belated declaration of war against Japan in August 1945), while American forces had moved into the south. In key respects, therefore, Korea was Asia's post-war 'Germany': a country ideologically divided by virtue of the disposition of Allied forces at the end of hostilities. The objective of a unified, independent Korea would not, it seemed, be easily achieved. In the five years following the Japanese surrender, both Moscow and Washington nurtured their own political clients in their respective areas of influence in Korea. Each big power supplied and trained the military forces of 'their' parts of the partitioned nation. In the north the Communist Party under Kim Il Sung became dominant, while in the south an election in May 1948 was won by the right-wing nationalist leader Syngman Rhee. Both North and South claimed sovereignty over the other in increasingly belligerent terms. A peaceful unification between equal partners now seemed impossible. The UN General Assembly with its automatic western majority recognized the regime in the South, though the Soviet veto in the Security Council prevented the admission of this 'Korea' to the organization. The first months of 1950 had seen increasing and increasingly serious incidents at the 38th parallel, the effective frontier dividing the country. Finally, on 25 June, the UN was informed of a full-scale invasion of the South by the North. The Security Council's initial discussion of the Korean crisis took place under one unusual condition which would affect the UN's entire approach to the issue. The Soviet delegation was absent from the meeting as part of a boycott of the Security Council in place since the beginning of 1950. The issue was the seating of Formosa (later known as Taiwan), whence the remnants of the Nationalist forces in China's civil war had fled after the victory of the Communists in 1949. This fragment of 'Chinese' sovereignty was, thanks to western dominance in the organization, accorded the status of sole legitimate representative of the country in the UN, a situation which would persist until the rapprochement between Washington and Beijing in 1971. The Security Council in June and July 1950 was, therefore, wholly western in composition and its decisions were not subject to Soviet veto. Whatever the short-term advantage the west might take of this, it carried a clear lesson about the futility of collective security in an ideologically polarized world [38; 53].

On 25 June a Security Council resolution called for the withdrawal of the northern forces back to the 38th parallel. The North, now embarked on an apparently unstoppable offensive, showed no inclination to comply with this essentially western appeal. Next, on 27 June a further Security Council resolution 'recommended' that UN members should assist South Korea against the northern invasion. In the meantime the United States had also responded unilaterally. The US Seventh Fleet was deployed between mainland China and Korea, and a series of naval bombardments and air-strikes was mounted against the invading forces. On 30 June American troops from the garrison forces in Japan were engaged in support of the South Korean army. This move was justified by Washington under the terms of Article 51 of the Charter, which permitted 'collective self-defence' [*Doc. 3(i)*]. Britain, Australia and New Zealand also signalled their intention to intervene. The western powers continued to use the freedom of initiative in the Security Council given to them because of the Soviet absence. An

Anglo-French resolution of 7 July called on all anti-North Korean forces to put themselves behind a 'Unified Command' which would fight under the UN flag. The United States was to provide the commander for this force who would 'report' to the Security Council. General Douglas MacArthur, the senior American general in Asia at this time, was thus appointed to command a 'UN force', which by the end of the following year would consist of contingents from seventeen states.

The deep flaws in this 'collective security' action were immediately evident. The Unified Command was not established under the terms of Article 43 of the Charter, which placed military obligations on all Charter signatories. It was, instead, an American initiative legitimized by a Security Council resolution [100 *p. 44*]. MacArthur remained an American officer answerable first of all to Washington and required only to 'inform' the Security Council. The 'multilateral' character of the undertaking was not enhanced by the fact that MacArthur was obviously politically ambitious and ideologically hawkish. The composition of the force was plainly western. It included nine of the thirteen members of the North Atlantic Treaty Organization (NATO), the western military alliance which had been formed the previous year. In addition, three 'white dominions' of the Commonwealth – Canada, Australia and New Zealand – were included. The remaining participants were drawn from American allies in Asia and Latin America. These resolutely western states made up only a minority of the Unified Command; two-thirds of the force was American [*Doc. 5*].

This western alliance had considerable early success. The Northern advance seemed inexorable throughout July and August and eventually reached the far south of the country. In mid-September, however, MacArthur launched a bold counter-attack by sea and air on Inchon, close to the South Korean capital, Seoul. Taken by surprise and now deprived of the strategic initiative, the Northern forces fell back and within a few weeks were close to the 38th parallel once again. But within this military success lay political danger for the west. Would the 'UN force' maintain its momentum by crossing into the North? From a supposedly impartial UN perspective this could hardly be acceptable. To counter-invade the North would transform a limited enforcement action into a war of conquest. Against this, however, were ranged a number of strategic and political considerations. From a strictly military viewpoint, it was argued, the initiative ought to be pursued and offensive momentum maintained. In the American view an occupation of the North by the 'UN' could prepare the way for the unification to which the organization was committed – on terms favourable to the west.

Circumstances in the Security Council had in the meantime changed significantly. On 1 August the Soviet Union not only resumed its participation but became (by rota) president of the Council. The free ride the west had enjoyed of decision-making unencumbered by the veto now shuddered to a halt. If the American-led force was to cross into the North it would not now do so on the basis of a new Security Council resolution. The crossing of the 38th parallel (to which MacArthur was enthusiastically committed) would have to be justified on the basis of existing Security Council mandates and on the support of the pro-western (and veto-free) General Assembly. Consequently, a western-sponsored resolution in the Assembly was passed on 7 October calling for the UN to establish stability 'throughout Korea'. This was taken by the US-led force as sufficient legitimization and it now followed its South Korean allies into the North. Already, at the beginning of October Beijing had warned that an invasion of the North by the 'UN' would be viewed by China as a threat to its own security. Now, as the western forces crossed the 38th parallel a large force of Chinese 'volunteers' forded the Yalu River which separates Manchuria from North Korea. Within weeks the fortunes of the war had been reversed once again and the UN was in headlong retreat from the North before the advancing Chinese.

If the claim of the original operation to the status of collective security was already weak, the American-led invasion of the North could have none. While the General Assembly had established its right (in Articles 10 and 11 of the Charter) to *discuss* issues of international security and make recommendations to the Security Council, it had no power to authorize enforcement. America now sought to resolve this problem to its own benefit by subverting one of the fundamental principles accepted during the original planning of the organization. Power was now given to the General Assembly in direct contradiction of the collective security mechanisms so delicately constructed at Dumbarton Oaks and San Francisco. In effect the United States arranged to move the constitutional goal-posts to serve its military and political objectives [91 *pp. 712–13*]. If the Charter gave the Soviet Union the power to block enforcement with its veto, the Charter could be changed. On 3 November 1950 the General Assembly passed the so-called 'Uniting for Peace' resolution by a large majority [88 *p. 20*]. Effectively an amendment to the Charter which reversed its original intent, this permitted the transfer of decisions over security measures to the General Assembly when action by the Security Council was blocked by a veto [*Doc. 6*]. A draft Security Council resolution that called on China to withdraw from Korea was now vetoed by the

Soviet Union only to be passed by the Assembly. The significance of this was somewhat blunted by the absence of any threat of military enforcement in the resolution. The UN was not now, in reality, in a position to make military threats nor carry them out. Events were taking their own course on the ground and the Security Council could do little to help or hinder them. Yet the circumstances from which the Uniting for Peace resolution emerged – and the institutional balance of power that ensured its adoption – were a further measure of the obstacles to effective collective security inherent in the international system of the early 1950s.

At the beginning of 1951 the military situation in Korea had switched yet again. The Chinese-North Korean forces, which had once more swept into the South, were checked and pushed back across the 38th parallel. Despite the availability of the Uniting for Peace process, the UN was now more cautious than it had been on the previous occasion about crossing into the North. MacArthur, whose actions and pronouncements had been causing growing unease among America's allies and in the White House itself, was summarily dismissed in April 1951. Henceforward western interests were re-defined and the 'war aim' of enforced unification quietly dropped. In this way the UN could adopt a posture more appropriate to a global security organization and appeared less compromised by the pursuit of western foreign policy objectives. After long and fraught negotiations an armistice was signed in July 1953. No final settlement based on unification or any other arrangement was reached, however. For the United Nations the Korean War simply provided the empirical proof of what its members and officials had come to accept: that collective security and cold war were incompatible. It also pointed up an inescapable secondary truth: that this situation could not be changed simply by the expedient of altering constitutional rules. The collective security system developed at Dumbarton Oaks and fine-tuned at San Francisco was probably the best available at that historical conjuncture, and if it could not work in its original form then a wholly different role would have to be found for the UN if the organization was to have any positive impact on the maintenance of international security [15; 29; 57; 60].

ANTECEDENTS OF PEACEKEEPING: PALESTINE AND KASHMIR

Some pointers towards such a role were, in fact, present before the Korean crisis. In two especially sensitive parts of the post-1945 world the United Nations had already established 'military' operations.

While not peacekeeping 'forces', these nevertheless exhibited some of the key characteristics of the peacekeeping project that would emerge in the coming years. In response to the major international conflicts that flared up firstly in Palestine and then in Kashmir, the UN established (in 1948 and 1949 respectively) international military observer missions. These operations were not designed to resolve the underlying conflicts in those areas between Israel and the Arab states over Palestine or between India and Pakistan over Kashmir. Their functions were merely to manage agreed cease-fires and to expedite political 'peacemaking'. There was no sense in which the Palestine and Kashmir interventions sought to enforce pre-determined collective security outcomes. There was, therefore, no requirement to identify one side or the other as an aggressor. This approach was facilitated by the fact that neither Palestine nor Kashmir was, in the late 1940s at least, an area of great east–west competition. Consequently, the Security Council was under no pressure to take a position on the merits and demerits of the political bases of the conflicts.

The United Nations Truce Supervision Organization (UNTSO) in Palestine was established in June 1948 in response to the outbreak of war between Israel and its Arab neighbours. This conflict had begun following a protracted period of political uncertainty and widespread though sporadic violence. The territory of Palestine had become the responsibility of the League of Nations after the dissolution of the Ottoman Empire at the end of the First World War. Its administration was 'mandated' by the League to Britain, which in the inter-war years sought to manage the conflicting demands of the Palestinian Arabs and the ever-increasing numbers of Jewish settlers from Europe. Then, after the end of the Second World War, Jewish immigration increased as the survivors of the Nazi holocaust made their way to their putative 'homeland'. Simultaneously, pressure grew for the formal establishment in Palestine of a Jewish political entity through the declaration of a new state of Israel. Britain, exhausted and enfeebled after 1945, was now confronted by a complex of political, military and emotional dilemmas in Palestine. It had little energy and no enthusiasm for resolving these and accordingly announced, in September 1947, that it was withdrawing from its mandate over the territory. The United Nations as the formal successor to the League had, therefore, no option but to assume responsibility. Initially both the United States and the Soviet Union agreed that the problem of Palestine should be dealt with by its partition into Jewish and Arab states. Although developments would soon change its perspective, at this time Moscow regarded a Jewish state established for the most part by European leftists as a potential diplomatic ally [83 *p. 169*]. On its side, the United States was under considerable domestic pressure from influential Jewish Americans to support such a state and, initially, seemed to respond to this. However, in early 1948, as the end of the British mandate approached, Washington appeared to change its mind and began to advocate the continuation of international administration through the creation of a UN Trusteeship. (In Africa and the South Pacific such Trusteeships had superseded the old League mandates in territories assumed to be still unprepared for independence.)

On 14 May 1948, in this climate of international uncertainty and intensifying local violence, the British mandate ended. The Jewish leadership immediately declared the creation of the state of Israel and war with the neighbouring Arab states followed. The Security Council responded with the appointment of a mediator, the Swedish aristocrat Count Folke Bernadotte. A fragile truce was hastily put together and Bernadotte established – with the participation of military officers from his native Sweden, the United States, Belgium and France – the UN Truce Supervision Organization. The Security Council resolution ordering this, in a rare reference to Chapter VII, warned that failure to comply with the cease-fire would risk enforcement action under Article 39. Despite this threat the original truce did not hold and fighting soon broke out with increased intensity. Bernadotte himself (along with a senior French member of UNTSO) was assassinated by Jewish extremists in September 1948 [*Doc. 7*]. UNTSO, however, expanded in both numbers (to nearly 600 in its early days) and in the range of national contributors. It became a permanent feature of the UN's peace efforts in the Middle East, surviving repeated crises in the region and contributing to the management of Arab-Israeli conflict over five decades [15; 47; 131].

The situation in Kashmir was similar to that in Palestine to the extent that it was rooted in issues of territorial division, emergent statehood and competing cultural and religious identities. The partition of British India into the independent states of India, which was predominantly Hindu, and Muslim Pakistan inevitably created border areas in which national and religious identity did not fully coincide. One such was the mountainous frontier territory of Jammu and Kashmir (generally referred to simply as Kashmir). Although almost entirely Muslim in population, its monarch (who had the status of a semi-autonomous ruler under the British) was Hindu and he opted for integration with India at independence. The result was an outbreak of fighting between the two already hostile new states immediately following independence. UN mediation eventually secured a cease-fire, which was to take effect from 1 January 1949. The cease-fire arrangements had been put in place by a commission established by the Security Council the previous year. Required to supervise and report on the effectiveness of this cease-fire, the commission sought the assistance of a body of military observers. The United Nations Military Observer Group in India and Pakistan (UNMOGIP) that grew out of this was modelled loosely on UNTSO, although it was much smaller, rarely exceeding 100 officers. Like UNTSO, it became a more or less permanent UN commitment in an inherently unstable area. In common with its Middle East counterpart it continued through repeated crises in the relationship of the protagonist states over the coming decades and made a clear if limited contribution to the management of these crises. As in the case of Palestine, the fact that the basic conflict over Kashmir continued unresolved was not of itself a failing on the part of UNMOGIP. Its role was one of peace observation and moral presence rather than active peacemaking. Once again, the operation represented an 'acceptable' level of military involvement for Security Council members, whose own foreign policies were not directly engaged with the problem but who nevertheless saw dangers in ignoring it [20; 159].

THE ADVENT OF PEACEKEEPING: SUEZ

In April 1953 the UN's first secretary-general, Trygve Lie from Norway, was succeeded by another Scandinavian, the Swedish diplomat Dag Hammarskjöld. Initially at least, Hammarskjöld seemed to bring a more neutral and 'institution-oriented' approach to his office than his predecessor. Lie's pro-western sympathies had been evident during the six years of his secretary-generalship [65 *p. 136*]. In contrast, Hammarskjöld's loyalty appeared to be to the organization first rather than to any national or bloc interests within it. Hammarskjöld's concern was to develop the UN as an impartial instrument of what he described as 'preventive diplomacy'. The first aim of the organization in this view should be to intervene actively in conflicts or potential conflicts *before* the question of a collective security response arose. His evident political detachment, combined with a cerebral approach to the problems of international politics, provided an initial impetus to the emergence of 'interpositionary' peacekeeping as an alternative to the enforcement of collective security originally envisaged in Chapter VII of the Charter. The second necessary element in the epiphany of peacekeeping was an actual crisis in which theory could be catalysed into practice. This presented itself in 1956 with the crisis surrounding Egypt's nationalization of the Suez Canal and the military reaction this provoked from Britain, France and Israel.

After the end of the 1948 war the fundamental conflicts of the region remained unresolved. Throughout the early 1950s tensions remained high. Egypt denied Israeli shipping access to the Suez Canal and encouraged Arab guerrilla (*fedayeen*) incursions across Israel's frontiers. By the beginning of 1956 the situation, particularly on the Egyptian border, had become so bad that Hammarskjöld himself spent several weeks in the region engaged in preventive diplomacy. He did not, however, meet with any obvious success.

Quite apart from its relations with Israel, Egypt faced other difficulties, both domestic and diplomatic, that affected its international behaviour. Under the presidency of Gammal Abdel Nasser, who took power in 1954 following an earlier military coup against the monarchy, Egypt was pursuing a distinctly nationalistic set of political objectives which had interrelated internal and external aspects. Domestically, Nasser sought to modernize and industrialize what he regarded as a backward-looking and tradition-bound Egypt. Internationally, he put himself forward as the natural leader of the Arab world as a whole, in particular the coalition of states confronting Israel. An important part of his modernization project for Egypt was the creation of the gigantic Aswan Dam, which was designed to provide irrigation and hydroelectric power for the entire Nile delta. The Aswan project was originally supposed to be funded by an international consortium led by the United States and involving the World Bank. In July 1956, however, Washington precipitately announced its withdrawal from the scheme. Nasser's diplomatic flirtation with the Soviet Union was being punished by the Republican administration of President Eisenhower (which had succeeded that of the Democrat Harry Truman in the presidential elections of 1952). Eisenhower's secretary of state, John Foster Dulles, was the driving force of the west's policy of 'containment' at this time. Accordingly, any threat of an expansion of Soviet influence into new areas such as the Arab world had to be robustly resisted. Threatened with the loss of a central component of his modernization programme and resentful at the west's apparent exploitation of the project in pursuit of cold war ends, Nasser made a characteristically dramatic gesture: the Suez Canal was nationalized. The Canal had originally been a French enterprise but a few years after its opening in 1869 Britain had bought a share in it and henceforward it had been the responsibility of an Anglo-French company. It had been designated an 'international waterway' open to the shipping of all nations by a treaty of 1888. The nationalization served a number of purposes for Nasser. It paid back the west for what was seen in Cairo as a breach of faith; it underlined the nationalist credentials of his regime by re-claiming 'national' territory; and it could be represented as a bold assertion of Afro-Asian rights by one of the emerging third world's natural leaders. Finally, the revenues from the Canal might go some way to providing an alternative source of funding for the Aswan project [43; 59].

Initially it seemed as though the west would simply absorb the impact of the nationalization. Dulles, although far from relaxed on international issues touching on the cold war, nevertheless sought to establish agreements on the management of the Canal while appearing to accept the fact of its change of ownership. The policy of containment might reasonably involve a corrective gesture towards those who would be Moscow's friends, but over-reaction could be counter-productive. The crisis appeared to be receding when, on 29 October, Israel launched a major attack on the Canal Zone. The Israeli assault was part of a broader conspiracy hatched by Britain and France following the nationalization. The second phase of the plan involved an ultimatum from London and Paris to 'both sides' in the fighting demanding their withdrawal from the Canal and their agreement to its 'protection' by an Anglo-French force. The ultimatum, as its authors were well aware, was wholly unacceptable to Nasser. Consequently, on 31 October, the RAF began bombing Egyptian positions in the Canal Zone and troop landings were to follow several days later. Egypt had, in the meantime, robbed the invasion of its supposed purpose by blocking the Canal with scuttled ships.

Washington, which had been deliberately kept in the dark over the Anglo-French manoeuvre, immediately saw through the pretence and reacted with considerable anger. A Security Council meeting on the crisis was immediately convened at America's request. Beyond a natural indignation at being so comprehensively disregarded by its NATO allies, US irritation also derived from sound cold war considerations [60 *p.* 224]. The Anglo-French adventure had exposed a basic contradiction between two cultural-historical strands in the western alliance: that between 'democrats' and 'imperialists'. The post-colonial spasm of the Suez invasion was, in American eyes, a disastrous blunder in a bipolar competition which was increasingly focused on winning the favour and support of the emerging, ex-colonial third world. More immediately, the Suez crisis dominated international attention at precisely the same time as Soviet tanks were crushing a popular anti-communist uprising in Hungary. What should have been an open goal *for* the west in the cold war propaganda game was thus turned into an own goal *by* the west. Nor did Eisenhower welcome the sense of diplomatic confusion and bungling brought by the crisis to his own domestic campaign for re-election which was underway at the time [158 *p. 18*]. In all, Suez was probably the worst intra-alliance crisis faced by the west in the five decades of the cold war. When the Security Council met on 30 October, an American draft resolution was put which called for an Israeli withdrawal. In a clear reference to Britain and France – which had not at that point engaged in military action – it also called on other UN members to refrain from interference. This provoked Britain's first ever Security Council veto, deployed, ironically, to block a resolution of its own alliance leader. Irony deepened when, as a result, the Uniting for Peace procedure was invoked with Soviet support to outflank this western veto. The issue now passed to the General Assembly. Despite the oddness of the bedfellows involved in moving the issue from the Security Council, it was a development which proved to be in the interest of the western bloc as a whole. In the more diffuse setting of the General Assembly the divisions between the European and American wings of the alliance were less obvious than in the starker forum of the Council. At all events, it was in the Assembly in the first three days of November that the outline of the UN's first peacekeeping force properly described began to emerge.

The key actor, in addition to Hammarskjöld himself, was the Canadian foreign minister, Lester Pearson. Pearson had long been associated with the institutional diplomacy of the UN, having been considered for appointment as its first secretary-general in 1945 before being rejected by Moscow as too pro-western. Beyond this, though, Canada was the other North American member of NATO and would clearly have been concerned at the breach which had opened between Washington and the leading European members of the alliance [*Doc. 8*]. The United States, while remaining in the background, itself encouraged moves towards a UN-based solution. On 4 November the General Assembly passed a Canadian resolution proposing the creation of an interpositionary United Nations Emergency Force (UNEF). Hammarskjöld quickly provided a preliminary plan for this. Pointing up for the first time what would become a fundamental principle of cold war peacekeeping, he suggested that the force should not include contingents from any of the permanent members of the Security Council [96 *p. 179*]. This would serve to immunize the situation against infection by larger international conflicts. His suggestion that the force commander should be the current UNTSO chief of staff, the Canadian General E.L.M. Burns, was therefore based on both practicality and principle. On 5 November the General Assembly authorized the establishment of the force. A more detailed plan was presented to the Assembly on 7 November, by which time British and French forces had occupied Port Said on the Canal. Further basic principles were laid down in this elaborated blueprint which would endure in peacekeeping practice long beyond the creation of UNEF. UNEF would not be used to coerce the host state. On the contrary, Egypt's consent to the intervention of UNEF and continuing acquiescence to its presence would be a fundamental condition of the operation. UNEF would be temporary, existing only as long as was necessary to achieve the objective of mutual disengagement of opposing forces and the stabilization of the general situation. It would have no role in altering the political or military conditions of the region. Nor would it have any internal power in the territories it operated in as it would be located only along agreed cease-fire lines. The costs of the operation would be borne by individual contributors. It was not, in short, to be a collective security undertaking designed to impose and enforce a particular outcome [17; 114; 131].

The Soviet Union, while happy to exploit the embarrassment of the west by using its own Uniting for Peace procedure against it, nevertheless remained concerned that the basic principle of Security Council primacy should not be lost through the precedent of UNEF. But, with a powerful Afro-Asian momentum behind the proposal for the force in the General Assembly, Moscow did not demur. Britain and France would have favoured a UN operation in which their own forces had a prominent role. This would have bolstered the particular interpretation of UNEF they wished to advance: that the UN force was completing a necessary job they themselves had begun. Both Hammarskjöld's proposal for a force free of great power involvement and the principle of Egyptian consent ruled this out. But neither London nor Paris was disposed to argue. The intensity of international condemnation of their attack on Egypt had taken them by surprise and, at least in Britain, the adventure had been hugely divisive domestically. The arrangement on offer provided Britain and France with as good a face-saving formula as they could reasonably hope for. Even if decision-making had remained within the Security Council, it is unlikely that they would have used their veto against the force.

For his part, Nasser was quick to appreciate – and then exploit – the power that the principle of 'host state consent' delivered to him [84 *p. 42*]. He had considerable leeway to shape both the functions and the composition of the force. UNEF's primary task, therefore, was understood to be the supervision of an Anglo-French-Israeli withdrawal. The nationality of its contributing forces was likewise influenced by Cairo's sensitivities. In all there were twenty-four offers of contingents, of which ten were initially accepted by Hammarskjöld. These all came from middle-range powers: Brazil, Canada, Colombia, Denmark, Finland, India, Indonesia, Norway, Sweden and Yugoslavia. Meanwhile, Nasser's evident – if conditional – co-operation with the UN was in sharp contrast to the reaction of Israel. There the government of prime minister David Ben-Gurion refused UNEF the necessary consent to operate on the national territory [158 *p. 22*]. The Suez affair of 1956 represented a further stage in a continuous deterioration in Israel's relations with the UN and its military interventions which had begun in the 1940s and continued for the next fifty years.

The first elements of UNEF arrived in the Canal Zone on 15 November 1956, barely two weeks after the crisis erupted. Within three months it had reached its maximum operational strength of 6,000. The British and French occupation forces had finally withdrawn just before Christmas 1956. The process of Israeli disengagement was slower but gradually progress was made. UNEF then remained in place until May 1967 when Egypt, exercising its right to withdraw its consent to the force's presence, brought the operation to an end [126 *pp. 30–1*]. Arab-Israeli tension had once again been increasing and the protagonists were preparing for what would become known as the Six-Day War. UNEF had in fact been running down for some time prior to 1967 as its main objectives were gradually achieved. In virtually all respects this first 'Hammarskjöldian' peacekeeping operation had been successful. It had performed the tasks assigned to it by the secretary-general *via* the General Assembly – for this was the real order of command, whatever the formal distribution of authority among UN organs might have suggested. It had done so by relying on interposition and moral authority rather than the use of force. Crucially, the operation had been free of entanglement in any significant east–west conflict. The Middle East in the late 1950s and early 1960s had not quite emerged as the major arena of bipolar conflict it became in subsequent years. In many ways, therefore, UNEF was the model for the UN's peacekeeping function in the cold war. It dampened and contained conflict in an area in which the superpowers did not (then) perceive core national interests to be engaged. The purpose of the operation in cold war terms was to maintain this situation.

THE 'PRINCIPLES' OF PEACEKEEPING

Before moving on to explore later crises and the UN operations mounted to deal with them during the cold war years, it is necessary to lay out more fully the conceptual basis of peacekeeping and the way it was represented by Hammarskjöld and his supporters. One way of approaching this is to place the basic propositions of peacekeeping against those of collective security as conceived by the planners of 1944 and 1945. The first point to make in this respect is that the legal basis of peacekeeping has none of the clarity of collective security, which, as we have seen, was fully set out in Chapter VII of the Charter. There has been some suggestion, *ex post facto*, that peacekeeping can be placed in the context of Chapter VI, 'Pacific Settlement of Disputes' [*Doc. 3(iii)*]. Certainly Article 34 gives the Security Council authority to 'investigate' any situation of 'international friction', while Article 36 allows it to 'recommend appropriate procedures or methods of adjustment'. But nowhere are the basic philosophy and mechanisms of peacekeeping referred to. Quite simply, preventive diplomacy and peacekeeping had not been envisaged when the Charter was being drafted. They emerged only when the machinery that had been placed at the centre of the UN's security aspirations had been rendered inoperable by global bipolarity. Hammarskjöld, originally appointed secretary-general as a safe if uninspired pair of diplomatic hands, acknowledged this paralysis of collective security and made the conceptual leap which permitted the UN to re-invent a viable military role for itself within the constraints of bipolarity [148; 162].

In October 1958 Hammarskjöld circulated to the General Assembly a 'Summary Study' of the experience derived from UNEF. This built on his initial reports in 1956 when the nature and character of the Suez operation was first determined. The Summary Study was as close as he was to come to providing a systematic statement of the concept of peacekeeping [*Doc. 9*]. While acknowledging that the Suez operation had a number of unique features that would not necessarily be replicated in future emergencies, Hammarskjöld sought to identify for the General Assembly 'certain basic principles and rules which would provide an adaptable framework for later operations which might be found necessary'. His purpose in this was to encourage the development of a framework of stand-by arrangements.

Firstly, peacekeeping was not 'the type of force envisaged under Chapter VII of the Charter'. There was, therefore, no legal obligation on either the host state or potential force contributors to comply with UN plans. Host state consent must be obtained. But this should not amount to 'host state interference' in the conduct of the operation. For this reason a detailed 'status of forces agreement' must be carefully negotiated and agreed. Some sensitivity would, though, be necessary to the host state's views on the composition of the force. With this in mind, the Summary Study proposed that as a general rule contributions should not come from the permanent members of the Security Council nor from any other state which 'might be considered as possibly having a special interest in the situation which has called for the operation'. As we have seen, UNEF was composed of contingents from what could be described as 'middle powers'. Henceforward the middle-power peacekeeper became a familiar player on the UN stage. 'Middle' had two connotations in the context of UN peacekeeping during the cold war. Firstly it related to capability. Clearly, peacekeeping contingents had to be sufficiently well-trained and resourced to carry out their mandate. But 'excessive' military capacity in a contributor could raise perceptions of threat on the part of protagonists in a crisis (thus Hammarskjöld's rejection of participation by the five permanent Security Council members). The trick, according to Lester Pearson, was to be 'big enough to discharge with effect the responsibilities we undertake [and] not big enough for others to fear us' [120 *p. 94*]. The second sense of 'middle' grows out of this. The peacekeeping participant ought also to occupy as nearly as possible an ideological mid-point between the cold war blocs. This would minimize the danger, real or perceived, of exposing a crisis to the bacterium of bipolar conflict. In fact, relatively few peacekeepers were 'neutral' in the strict, international legal sense. Only Sweden and Finland in the initial composition of UNEF, and Ireland and Austria in several later operations, were actually 'neutral' constitutionally speaking. But other states, despite being formally aligned with international blocs, had a sufficiently respected international standing to permit their participation. In this way Canada, Denmark and Norway, although members of NATO, were acceptable in UNEF and several subsequent operations.

Beyond the identity of contributors, a number of operational bench-marks established by UNEF should also, in Hammarskjöld's view, be adopted as general principles. One of these was freedom of movement for the peacekeeping force within its agreed operational area. This had been a central component of the UN's status of forces agreement with Egypt. At the same time, UN forces must not attempt to exercise authority either in competition with the host state or in joint operations with it. Such a situation would expose the UN to the danger of involvement in internal politics (which was expressly prohibited by the Charter). In this UNEF was a poor guide to future practice. In the specific circumstances of the Suez crisis non-involvement was easily maintained. This would not be the case in future undertakings, however, and the issue of the peacekeepers' impact on local political developments would become a major problem for the conduct of UN peacekeeping in a range of operations. It was to present itself in a particularly vivid and complex form in the UN's next major commitment, that in the Congo. The Summary Study broached another central problem of the peacekeeping concept: the use of force by the UN. Hammarskjöld took it as 'understood' that peacekeeping operations 'could never include combat activity'. Contributing forces would, however, have the natural right to self-defence. It was essential that the circumstances under which this right could be exercised be strictly defined if its interpretation was not to 'blur the distinction between [peacekeeping] operations ... and combat operations, which would require a decision under Chapter VII of the Charter'. Here too the experience of Suez was not sufficiently representative to be generally applicable. Once again it would be the Congo operation between 1960 and 1964 that would expose the fragility of Hammarskjöld's design.

Finally, the Summary Study confronted another area of considerable contention in the future: the financing of operations. Could peacekeeping – an activity not conceived of at the founding of the organization and not obviously located within the Charter – be considered a 'normal' cost of the UN and therefore supported by the regular budget? For Hammarskjöld it clearly should be: as activities 'based on decisions of the General Assembly or Security Council [peacekeeping] expenses should be allocated in accordance with the normal scale of contributions'. In short, they should be an obligatory expense for all UN members. This was a point of controversy even in 1956. The Soviet Union, in line with its long-standing approach to the distribution of power in the UN, argued that only the Security Council could impose costs on members. UNEF, as a product of the Uniting for Peace procedure, was a General Assembly undertaking. From a different perspective, some Arab states took the position that Britain, France and Israel had 'caused' the expense of UNEF as a result of their aggression. On the principle that the 'aggressor pays', they should be responsible for the costs of the operation. These were, though, relatively mild opening exchanges in what would develop into a full-scale crisis over authorization and financing in later years [11; 110; 127].

Key Contrasts between Collective Security and Peacekeeping

	Collective security	Peacekeeping
Precondition for action	Identification of aggressor	Identification of crisis
Nature of mandate	Enforcement	Interposition and observation
Contributing forces	Big powers	Middle and small powers
Basis of participation	Charter obligation (Art. 43)	Voluntary participation
Control	Security Council	Security Council or General Assembly
Method	Exercise of military force	Assertion of moral force
Relationship to protagonists	Imposed	Agreement ('host state consent')
Objective	Securing of pre-determined outcome	Creation of conditions for negotiated settlement

The evident and early success of the Suez operation did not, paradoxically, serve the larger peacekeeping venture well. Hammarskjöld was anxious to capitalize on the experience of Suez in order to establish the broader concept of peacekeeping. As a result he risked building too great a superstructure on the fairly shallow foundations of this single and in some ways unrepresentative experience. UNEF was born of an unusual consensus between the superpowers (Soviet misgivings over its General Assembly authorization notwithstanding). The operation had clearly defined and achievable objectives which did not drift amidst changing circumstances. The protagonists on both sides were happy enough to accept UN intervention as providing, respectively, vindication or cover for disengagement. And these actors were all sovereign states, well established within international society. As such they provided reliable interlocutors for the UN, being conscious of their international standing and the importance of national prestige. Operationally UNEF was contained within a clearly demarked zone (around the Canal) with a firmly delimited purpose. It could not, therefore, easily stray, either physically or metaphorically, into the internal politics of the host state. At no stage did UNEF approach the border line between self-defence and combat because it did not face situations where self-defence was a consideration.

No subsequent peacekeeping operation would demonstrate these text-book characteristics. It was Hammarskjöld's error, though perhaps without benefit of hindsight an understandable one, to assume that they would. In the meantime, most member states of the UN seemed content to accept the assumptions of its activist secretary-general. In consequence a dangerously complacent 'leave it to Dag' mentality began to take hold which would complicate ensuing developments in peacekeeping.

3 THE 1960s: PEACEKEEPING INSTITUTIONALIZED

As the evident success of UNEF entered international political consciousness, high expectations of the UN soon became the norm. These were further encouraged by the continuing work of the previously established observer missions in Palestine and Kashmir. UNTSO continued its work in tandem with UNEF on Israel's borders and UNMOGIP maintained its presence in the now peaceful mountains between India and Pakistan. It was in this relatively up-beat atmosphere that a new UN operation was mounted in June 1958. A crisis in the internal politics of Lebanon which had evident international implications led to the deployment of a UN military observer mission. The United Nations Observation Group in Lebanon (UNOGIL) was established in response to a sharp deterioration of inter-ethnic relations in Lebanon's volatile patchwork of religions and cultures. The general atmosphere in the Middle East region had been more than normally unsettled after the declaration in February 1958 of the 'unification' of Egypt and Syria to create the United Arab Republic (UAR). Lebanon's Maronite Christian president, Camille Chamoun, was deeply worried at this apparent threat of a Muslim Arab hegemony throughout the Middle East. Internal disorder in Lebanon during May was claimed by Chamoun to be externally generated and a threat to Lebanon's pro-western, anti-Arab nationalist position. He therefore enlisted the assistance of the still western-dominated UN to protect Lebanon from infiltration and what he perceived as a threat of invasion by neighbouring Syria, now part of the new, apparently mighty UAR [42 *p. 239*].

The danger of a Soviet veto caused Chamoun to dilute his original demand for a full-scale UN force to protect his borders, but the circumstances within which UNOGIL had to operate deteriorated dramatically just a few weeks after its initial deployment. In mid-July

1958 the Iraqi monarchy was overthrown by radical nationalists. Western fears about pan-Arab militancy first provoked by the creation of the UAR now deepened. The United States, aware of the pro-Soviet (or at least distinctly anti-western) tendencies of Arab nationalism at this time, launched a pre-emptive 'invasion' of Lebanon. Some 14,000 US troops were landed and this in turn raised pressure on the UN to increase its presence in order to 'fence-off' the conflict from super-power rivalry. UNOGIL's strength was now raised to nearly 600 and its operations on the Syrian border were extended. The crisis had passed before the end of 1958 and UNOGIL was withdrawn in December after a deployment of only six months. In reality, the danger of international conflict in the Lebanon in 1958 had probably been over-stated by Chamoun for his own internal political reasons. But it was characteristic of the climate of the time that the United States was ready to take it seriously enough to engage in extensive military action. In this environment the utility of even an observation mission by the UN was clear. UNOGIL's prior presence appeared to constrain the action of the United States after it had landed its troops. It helped to ensure that these troops remained concentrated near their beachheads rather than being deployed to flashpoints where their presence might have provoked more problems than it solved. The UN presence also provided a cover for the withdrawal of these American forces – just as UNEF had for those of Britain and France in Suez (though in rather different circumstances) [133 *p. 289*]. It appeared two years into the life of UNEF, another victory for preventive diplomacy and the peacekeeping method. A sharp corrective to this mounting optimism was soon to be administered [114; 131].

PEACEKEEPING UNDER STRAIN: THE CONGO

On 30 June 1960 Belgium withdrew from its vast African colony, the Congo (renamed Zaire in 1966 before reverting to Democratic Republic of Congo in 1997). The independence of this huge, ethni-cally diverse territory came precipitately and without any semblance of proper preparation by the decolonizing power. In January 1960, following disturbances during the previous year, Belgium announced its intention to withdraw and to transfer power to an independent African government within six months. Apprehensive of the political and security dangers inherent in a protracted pre-independence phase and uncertain of its capacity to manage them, Belgium had reacted with something like panic to the first stirrings of African nationalism. The consequences of such a rushed and ill-prepared process for the newly independent state, if considered at all, played no significant part in the calculations of Brussels. With no more than a handful of university graduates and no doctors, lawyers or trained military officers, the emergent state was courting disaster from the moment of its independence.

It was not wholly unexpected then when on 12 July, within two weeks of independence, the Congo's prime minister, Patrice Lumumba, and its president, Joseph Kasavubu, sought UN help to deal with a major crisis in the authority of the new state. The recently formed national army, the *Armée Nationale Congolese* (ANC), had mutinied against its European officers and a chaotic spasm of looting and rape had ensued. In response Belgium sent a force of paratroops, primarily to protect the still considerable European population. Exploiting the chaos in the national capital, Leopoldville (later Kinshasa), the leader of the mineral-rich southern province of Katanga, Moise Tshombe, declared his own 'independence' from the Congo. This attempted secession had been, at least in the view of the central government, connived at by Belgium and France. The European powers had, by this account, subverted Congolese politics in an attempt to safeguard their neo-colonial commercial and industrial interests in the province. From the outset it should have been clear that UN involvement in the Congo would be much more complex and dangerous than it had been in Suez. There were four separate problems to be confronted initially. Firstly, the withdrawal of the recently returned Belgian forces had to be effected. But this was relatively straightforward compared to the other challenges facing any multilateral intervention. Public order had to be restored; the ANC had to be properly trained and inculcated with military discipline to prevent a repetition of the crisis; and the state had to be re-unified and separatism discouraged. The inapplicability of Hammarskjöld's Suez-inspired peacekeeping concept in such a situation should have been evident. 'Host state consent' had only limited meaning where control of the state was uncertain and contested. Clearly, the issue of the self-defence of the UN force and how it was to be distinguished from active combat would be thrown wide open if the UN was to be responsible for the imposition of order. Most delicately, perhaps, the principle of non-interference in local politics was simply unsustainable if the UN was to act on behalf of the central government against regional secession. Finally, the crisis in the Congo had international implications that were potentially profound. Lurking behind the post-colonial machinations of the Europeans was the danger that the crisis would be re-shaped into a broader east–west confrontation [40; 102].

The issue was brought to the Security Council by Hammarskjöld himself. He did this by invoking for the first time in the organization's history the power given to the secretary-general under Article 99 of the Charter. Hammarskjöld initially sought Security Council authorization for an operation that would cover the withdrawal of Belgian forces from the Congo. At this point the aims of the intervention were familiar. The principle was similar to that of UNEF in its 'replacement' of the Anglo-French invaders of Suez and to a lesser extent of UNOGIL in its constraint of American action in Lebanon. Profound complications would not be long in coming, however. For now, Tunisia, which was one of the non-permanent members of the Security Council at the time, produced an enabling resolution which established a force to provide 'assistance' to the Congolese government. The resolution also called for a withdrawal of Belgian forces, though it stopped short of overt criticism of Brussels. In an early intimation of future divisions, both France and Britain abstained in the vote, though they stopped short of a veto [*Doc. 10(i)*]. The force to be assembled became known as ONUC, an acronym of its French initials, *Opération des Nations Unies au Congo*. It would outstrip in size and ambition any UN project undertaken hitherto. It would last for four years and involve major contributions from seventeen states with lesser participation by another nineteen. At its peak its personnel would reach almost 20,000.

Hammarskjöld embraced the challenge of the Congo with considerable enthusiasm. It was, in some respects, a natural extension of the peacekeeping project beyond the international issues that had been characteristic of the 1950s. During that decade the problems of the Middle East and Arab nationalism had dominated peacekeeping efforts. Now, at the beginning of the 1960s, the new international challenges would, it seemed, come from the emergence of independent black Africa. Yet the 'international' justifications for the UN's intervention in the Congo were not, at the outset, especially strong [158 *p. 51*]. Certainly, Leopoldville's initial request related to 'Belgian aggression' against a new, independent state, but this was a symptom and not the cause of the fundamental problem. The danger of cold war internationalization, although to develop later, was not obvious in mid-1960. Lumumba had first approached both the United States and the Soviet Union for bilateral help before being directed by each of them to the United Nations. Hammarskjöld's perception of the 'international' in the Congo probably derived from his general view of the UN's responsibility for the management of the international state system as a whole. In 1960 the strains on this system derived from its rapid expansion through the process of decolonization. In this view, the pressures on the new international entities emerging from this process should, therefore, be a major subject for UN attention. This inclusive definition of what was properly 'international' allowed the circumvention of the basic Charter principle – embodied in Article 2(7) – of non-intervention 'in matters which are essentially within the domestic jurisdiction of any state'. From the outset Hammarskjöld's 'systemic' view of ONUC's purposes cut across the more immediate and local perspectives of Patrice Lumumba. The Congolese prime minister, understandably enough, insisted that the UN's primary role should be to bolster the authority of his government in Leopoldville. This, after all, had been the basis of his original approach to the UN. These differing perceptions led quickly to conflict between Leopoldville and New York [10; 96].

Beyond this clash of perspectives there were political constraints on the capacity of ONUC to deliver what Lumumba sought. Belgium was reluctant to withdraw its forces before the internal situation in the Congo had stabilized and it was inconceivable that the Security Council, subject to western veto, would vote to take any strong measures against a member of the western alliance. Britain and France had already abstained on the original vote to establish ONUC and would hardly have supported any direct confrontation between the UN and Belgian forces. Yet, in pursuing the restoration of order that would bring a Belgian withdrawal, UN forces were engaged in the disarming of the Congo's own national army. If this were not bad enough, relations between the UN and Leopoldville were damaged further by the secession of Katanga. Encouraged by Belgian officers in its paramilitary 'gendarmerie' and by locally based western diplomats, Katanga's defiance of the central government continued unchallenged by ONUC in the first months of its operations. To move against Katanga, Hammarskjöld insisted, would go beyond the 'peacekeeping' mandate and take the UN into the area of 'enforcement' [135 *p. 234*]. All this amounted in the view of Lumumba and his radical nationalist supporters to a betrayal of the UN's original promise. Beyond the Congo itself this perception of ONUC as an instrument of 'imperialism' was increasingly echoed in other third world states and was beginning to strike an opportunistic chord with the Soviet Union.

This potentially disastrous situation worsened dramatically at the beginning of September 1960 when the central government fell into constitutional chaos. A long-standing and barely suppressed rivalry between Lumumba and President Kasavubu had been aggravated by Lumumba's increasingly anti-western rhetoric. Kasavubu, more amenable to western blandishments, decided to dismiss his prime minister. Lumumba responded in kind by 'dismissing' the president. Caught in the middle, ONUC was made aware of the extent to which, like it or not, it had become a major actor in the Congo's internal politics. Two fatal operational decisions were now taken by Andrew Cordier, Hammarskjöld's representative in Leopoldville. He ordered the closure of all airfields in the country and shut down the capital's radio station. The effect of these moves was to favour Lumumba's enemies. By grounding air traffic the UN prevented the transfer to the capital of troops loyal to the prime minister from his power base in Stanleyville, capital of Orientale province. By closing the radio station Lumumba was denied his only means of mass communication while Kasavubu was able to broadcast from the capital of the 'friendly' former French Congo, Brazzaville, just across the Congo river [96 *p. 445*].

The extent to which these steps were intentionally anti-Lumumbist is impossible to judge with any certainty. But Cordier was an American and indeed almost all of Hammarskjöld's key representatives in the Congo at this time were westerners [84 *p. 248*]. The so-called 'Congo Club' of advisers to the secretary-general in New York was similarly bereft of communist bloc members. This was indicative of the essentially western cultural assumptions which underpinned the concept of 'impartial' peacekeeping. The inescapable fact was that the peacekeeping idea itself had no obvious place in Soviet views of international relations and their management at this time. Over Suez, where UN intervention had little impact on the bipolar contest and where it delivered a bonus of intra-western embarrassment, Moscow was content to acquiesce in the process. As the Congo crisis took on ideological and diplomatic dimensions which impinged directly on the central cold war conflict, however, the Soviet Union began to take a close critical interest in what was being done in the Security Council's name [14 *pp. 482–3*]. And, with the best will towards impartiality in the world, the western managers of peacekeeping would always be at risk of bringing their own cultural and ideological assumptions, however unconsciously, to their operational decisions.

Cordier was replaced immediately after the airport and radio station affair (supposedly in a routine change-over) by an Indian national, Rajeshwar Dayal, who brought a greater third world sensibility to the post [102 *pp. 77–8*]. But the Soviet Union had picked up on the issue and now used it to attack what it insisted was pro-western bias in the upper echelons of ONUC. In the Security Council in mid-September the Soviet representative denounced the failure of the operation to

confront 'imperialism' in the Congo and pointed to the preponder-
ance of western personnel at its head. The impression of a UN
machine working against radical third world aspirations (here personified by Patrice Lumumba) was becoming widespread among the Afro-
Asian bloc in the UN. The always thin fiction of non-interference by
the UN in the Congo's politics became even more threadbare with the
waning of Lumumba's power. The Soviet Union, disregarding the
complexities of the secretary-general's own position, held him personally responsible for what it alleged was a western conspiracy in the
Congo. This was, to a degree, an inevitable consequence of the 'leave
it to Dag' culture which had grown out of the Suez operation and
which Hammarskjöld himself had, however unwittingly, tended to
encourage. His close personal identification with the development of
the general philosophy and operational details of peacekeeping could
now be turned against him. More particularly, his utilization of the
considerable initiative permitted to him under Article 99 of the Charter
in the establishment of ONUC meant that whatever the real limits of
his personal control over the politics of either the UN or the Congo,
he would be a prime target for the side which perceived itself as the
loser from the UN intervention.

On 23 September 1960 the Soviet leader Nikita Khrushchev himself addressed the Security Council on ONUC's shortcomings and the
controversial nature of its political direction. After denouncing the
failure of the UN to confront the secession of Katanga and excoriating its
supposed anti-Lumumba manoeuvres earlier in the month, Khrushchev
laid a proposal for radical reform before the Council [*Doc. 11*]. The
office of secretary-general concentrated too much power in the hands
of one individual, he argued, and therefore should be abolished.
'There are neutral nations', he said, 'but no neutral men' [84 *p. 204*].
Hammarskjöld's Swedish nationality did not make Hammarskjöld
himself 'neutral'. The office should, therefore, be replaced by a
'troika' (triumvirate) composed of representatives of three distinct
groups of states: western, communist and Afro-Asian. This would
ensure that neither of the cold war blocs could exploit the power of
the office. Such a reform would, therefore, ensure a truly internationalized United Nations. It would also, of course, dispense with the concept
of an institutional bureaucracy loyal to the institution rather than the
national origins of its personnel. The tradition of the international
civil servant that had developed in the League of Nations would thus
be abandoned. The *troika* system would, in short, have formalized the
bipolar structure of the cold war international system into a permanent feature of the UN's architecture.

In the event, there was little support for the *troika* proposal. The opposition of the west could be taken for granted, but, crucially, few third world countries seemed to be enthused by the idea either [84 p. 206]. Whatever their misgivings over the direction of the Congo operation, the Afro-Asians nevertheless saw in Hammarskjöld a figure committed to the UN as an institution rather than either of the two cold war blocs which sought to dominate it. Hammarskjöld himself was able to exploit this feeling in his own defence when he replied to Khrushchev's proposals [96 p. 461]. The latter, sensing the mood against him, quietly dropped them [*Doc. 12*]. With a bitter ideological dispute developing at this time between Moscow and Beijing (the incipient 'Sino-Soviet split'), the mood of the Afro-Asian bloc was of considerable concern to the Soviet leadership. Yet important issues were raised by the *troika* affair and it revealed some significant truths about the nature of the UN at this dangerous point in the cold war. Firstly, the plain fact was that the senior and most sensitive strata of the UN secretariat were indeed populated disproportionately by western officials. The balance of bureaucratic power – and therefore control of much day-to-day decision-making – was in implicitly anti-Soviet hands. The extent to which this personnel really represented bloc interests was obviously debatable, but Soviet suspicions, fuelled by a Marxist sense of the individual as agent of class (or sectional or bloc interests) were understandable. Secondly, it was now evident that peacekeeping, which was designed to prevent cold war involvement in peripheral areas of bipolar competition, could actually become the *focus* of such involvement. As Ernest Lefever put it, the UN 'did not ... keep the cold war out of the Congo. On the contrary, it further politicised the crisis and ensured that the cold war would be fought in that chaotic arena' [137 p. 207]. Paradoxically, cold war competition now posed a considerable threat to the idea of peacekeeping – which had itself developed to take the edge off that competition. The Congo illustrated something not evident over Suez: that dangerous situations can deteriorate despite *or even because* of UN intervention. The Congo of September 1960 was not the Congo of July 1960. The political environment had altered fundamentally and the danger of cold war involvement had increased dramatically in consequence. Once committed, however, ONUC had no option but to adapt as best it could to rapidly changing circumstances.

Meanwhile, as the *troika* issue was argued out in New York, in the Congo itself it was unclear who exactly constituted the central government. Both Kasavubu and Lumumba sought legitimacy by sending their own separate delegations to the General Assembly, which initially declined to seat either. Confusion deepened in mid-September when the ANC commander, Colonel Joseph Mobutu, announced an army coup and proceeded to expel Soviet and other eastern bloc diplomats from Leopoldville. Moscow was not alone in scenting western connivance in this conveniently anti-Soviet turn of events and Afro-Asian concern over the drift of events increased. For Hammarskjöld the immediate danger was that Lumumba would be provoked into inviting a direct Soviet intervention. A suspiciously rapid rapprochement between Mobutu and Kasavubu, however, forced Lumumba onto the defensive. He had now, humiliatingly, to place himself under UN protection as his Congolese enemies moved against him [40; 102].

In November 1960 the General Assembly, with considerable encouragement from the western bloc, finally accepted the credentials of the Kasavubu delegation. This effectively legitimized the Mobutu–Kasavubu regime in Leopoldville. It also marked a reversal of the UN's previous commitment to seek conciliation between Kasavubu and Lumumba. This apparent western victory was not welcomed by Hammarskjöld but he could not avoid being identified with the whole process [96 *p. 478*]. The decision to accept the credentials of the anti-Lumumba faction triggered a sequence of events in the Congo which would make Hammarskjöld's position – and that of ONUC on the ground – even more difficult. Responding to his defeat in New York Lumumba slipped away from his UN protectors in Leopoldville. His aim was to reach his Stanleyville power base where he hoped to rally sufficient support to mount a challenge to the new regime. He was captured by Mobutu's ANC *en route*. A few weeks later, in January 1961, the central government, now firmly under Mobutu's control, handed its prisoner over to Tshombe's 'government' in Katanga. There Lumumba was quickly and brutally murdered, an outcome which had probably been pre-arranged between Mobutu and Tshombe. The consequences for ONUC were immediate. The shortcomings in ONUC's protection for Lumumba in Leopoldville had been bad enough, its failure to prevent his transfer to Katanga and subsequent murder seemed to suggest at the minimum a culpable negligence. Although no convincing suggestion of UN complicity in Lumumba's fate was ever made, persistent and credible reports later claimed that the US Central Intelligence Agency (CIA) was deeply involved in the affair through its influence over Mobutu [30 *p. 198*]. Indonesia, the UAR and Morocco now withdrew their contingents from ONUC in protest and others threatened to follow suit. The UAR and Guinea also formally recognized a rival 'central government' declared by Lumumba's supporters in Stanleyville [84 *p. 264*]. The Soviet Union once again demanded Hammarskjöld's dismissal.

As a direct consequence of Lumumba's death and the political chaos which surrounded it, the Security Council authorized a new, more robust mandate for ONUC. On 21 February 1961 it was authorized to use force if necessary to prevent civil war [*Doc. 10(ii)*]. This represented an abandonment of the basic Hammarskjöldian principle that peacekeepers should use force only in self-defence and only then with great circumspection. More significantly, perhaps, the new mandate meant that ONUC now had an enforcement function, albeit a negative one, in the requirement placed on it to prevent civil war by military means. This was the first, formal acknowledgement of a phenomenon which would much later, in the post-cold war era, be characterized as 'mission creep'. Despite misgivings on Hammarskjöld's part, the new mandate improved ONUC's international credibility. The superpower relationship within which it was required to operate had also changed for the better. In January 1961 President John F. Kennedy moved into the White House, bringing with him a greater sensitivity to African and other third world feelings than that demonstrated by the Eisenhower administration [24; 28].

Whatever the circumstances, Congolese and international, surrounding the murder of Lumumba, his death permitted the consolidation of the Mobutu–Kasavubu government in Leopoldville. This brought some stability to the situation at the centre. Consequently, the UN could now give greater attention to the issue of Katanga, a problem that would dominate the remainder of ONUC's operations in the Congo. While the rest of the country had been struggling through the successive crises of army mutiny, foreign intervention and violent political factionalism, secessionist Katanga had remained free from close attention from the UN, though ONUC troops were stationed there [102 *p. 45*]. ONUC's position in relation to Katanga remained opaque during the first year of its presence in the Congo. Katanga's claims to independence had been favoured by the contrast between the chaos elsewhere in the Congo and its own evident prosperity, efficient administration and political tranquillity [133 *p. 298*]. Its fundamental reliance on external support from both European and white African states was apparent, however. Although armed with its supposedly more effective mandate after February 1961, and with the great majority of UN members hostile to Katanga, it was never clear whether ONUC was specifically authorized to end its secession by force. Could such a course of action reasonably be interpreted as 'preventing civil war'? The Security Council itself could not possibly agree on this and the question was never resolved. The continuing ambiguity led to the UN's next major crisis in the Congo – and to the death of Hammarskjöld.

The secretary-general himself seemed not to favour the maximalist interpretation of the UN's mandate in regard to Katanga. By mid-1961 he had been relieved of much of the Soviet and radical Afro-Asian pressure which had surrounded the *troika* debates and the murder of Lumumba. He now sought to pull ONUC as far as possible towards a 'peacekeeping' role within his own conception of the term. Certainly the cold war dimension to the Congo question was less marked than previously as both Moscow and Washington (with Kennedy in office) were now committed to a unified Congo. But the absence of obvious superpower conflict could not of itself create conditions for Suez-style interpositionary peacekeeping. The internal situation in the Congo remained highly volatile, with no agreed political consensus among the factions. There was, therefore, no peace for ONUC to keep. Even with the more stark cold war tensions muted, the UN's position therefore remained complex and dangerous. Throughout the first half of 1961 the Katangese regime defied all UN attempts to negotiate its reintegration into the Congo. Its heavily armed gendarmerie, led by European officers and backed by foreign mercenaries, was in reality more of an army than a police force. Tshombe and his European advisers, therefore, were largely unmoved by the diplomatic urgings of the UN [102; 113].

In August, following mounting tension between United Nations personnel and the Katangese forces in the capital Elisabethville, a major crisis erupted. Hammarskjöld's local representative, the young Irish diplomat Conor Cruise O'Brien, who was determined to cut through the separatist regime's temporizing and provocations, had ordered ONUC forces to arrest and expel foreign military personnel [*Doc. 13*]. The ill-planned operation was unsuccessful and turned into another humiliation for the UN in Katanga. Buoyed by his evident victory over ONUC, Tshombe became even more intractable. In response O'Brien, with support from ONUC headquarters in Leopoldville, ordered a second, more forceful operation by UN forces in Elisabethville a few weeks later. In the flush of the initial success of this second operation O'Brien, foolishly and fatally, announced the end of Katanga's secession. There was an immediate international reaction. This was not what the UN membership had assumed to be happening. The ambiguity of the February resolution had not been resolved in a way that would permit the UN to extinguish the secession of Katanga by force. The western members of the Security Council in particular were angry at not having been consulted. Two incompatible versions of events now emerged. O'Brien, with some support from UN officials in Leopoldville, claimed that Hammarskjöld had given prior approval to the operation. The secretary-general, through his aides in New York, insisted on the contrary that the operation had been conceived and organized locally. It would not, they insisted, have been approved in New York had they been consulted [16; 40; 96].

In the face of a deeply hostile diplomatic reaction in the west and with the secretary-general himself apparently disassociating himself from it, the anti-secessionist operation petered out. Its early momentum was not maintained, it had failed to achieve its strategic objectives and had succeeded only in increasing tensions in Katanga. For Hammarskjöld personally the crisis must have brought a huge intensification of the stress he had been working under virtually from the start of the Congo operation [*Doc. 14*]. He now flew to the Congo in an attempt to rescue the situation. After consultations in Leopoldville he arranged to meet Tshombe in neighbouring Northern Rhodesia whence the Katangese leader had fled when the latest UN operation began. On the evening of 17 September 1961 Hammarskjöld was killed when his plane crashed *en route* to this meeting [84; 96].

Hammarskjöld's death did not bring any fundamental change to the character of the UN operation in the Congo. His replacement, however, was the UN's first non-European secretary-general, the Burmese diplomat U Thant. His Afro-Asian identity was to prove significant. The furore surrounding ONUC's moves against Katanga in August and September had been generated by western powers. Although the sharpest edges of cold war conflict had declined over the Congo in the course of 1961, international cleavages persisted. The division now was, loosely, one between the European 'imperialists' (France, Belgium and Britain) on the pro-Katanga side and the Afro-Asian world on the other. The United States, although angered at the lack of consultation over ONUC's military operations in Katanga in August and September, was now ranged against its European allies on this 'colonial' issue. More substantially, the pro-Katangese westerners were confronted by the increasingly cohesive 'non-aligned' bloc, which objected not to military action by the UN against Katanga but its failure. The new secretary-general's third world background went some way to easing the pressure of this grouping on the UN itself [19].

In the aftermath of the August–September crisis and Hammarskjöld's death, a new Security Council resolution was adopted in

November with further implications for ONUC's mandate. The UN now committed itself to an even more forceful approach than that of the February resolution. ONUC was instructed to take 'vigorous action', including the use of force, to end Katangese secession [*Doc. 10(iii)*]. Following this the UN's intervention in the Congo moved towards its endgame. Sporadic outbreaks of fighting from late 1961 until the end of 1962 finally left the UN – now reinforced with a large and effective Indian component – in control of Katanga. The Congo was once again unified under a centralized administration in Leopold-ville. The confusing and apparently capricious cross-currents of Congolese politics now saw Tshombe appointed prime minister of the unified state. Real power, however, lay with Mobutu, who formalized his authority when he displaced Kasavubu as head of state in 1965. In the meantime, ONUC had withdrawn from the Congo in June 1964. Mobutu remained in power for more than three decades, being ousted only in 1997 shortly before his death. His regime, over the birth of which the United Nations had presided, was one of the most inefficient and corrupt in the world. The longevity of this 'kleptocracy' was due in no small part to Mobutu's continuing loyalty to western interests, a loyalty first demonstrated in the critical months of 1960.

BACK ON TRACK? FROM NEW GUINEA TO CYPRUS

Regardless of the strains placed on UN peacekeeping by the Congo experience (including the violent death of its pioneer), the basic concept of military interposition proved robust enough to survive. Throughout the 1960s new observer and peacekeeping operations based on the precepts which emerged at the time of Suez continued to be established in various parts of the world. Typically, these operations were designed to meet crises on the periphery of superpower interests. That is to say, problems marginal to the central ideological and geographical balance of the cold war. They were not in the same category as, for example, Berlin, Hungary or Cuba. In these areas of core interest the superpowers reserved the right to pursue their own interests unencumbered by any multilateral interference. UN involvement was acceptable and desirable to the superpowers where, as in the Middle East or the Congo, cold war alignments were present but in a latent form.

One such commitment, the considerable scope of which has perhaps been obscured by its geographical remoteness from the centres of global power, was in West New Guinea. Colonial administration had continued in this part of the old Dutch East Indies after the Netherlands had withdrawn from the rest of the huge archipelago that had constituted its Asia Pacific empire. The Melanesian people of the physically wild and diverse territory of West New Guinea had little in common with Indonesia, the successor state to the rest of the Dutch East Indies. They showed no enthusiasm for exchanging rule from Europe for rule from Jakarta. The radical nationalist regime of President Sukarno in Indonesia was, however, determined to complete the territorial transfer from the Dutch by taking control of West New Guinea (or 'Irian Jaya' as the Indonesians called it). The Netherlands, while generally benign in its rule of the territory, had done little to develop its people or its natural resources. This failure, along with the general decolonizing spirit of the 1950s and 1960s, deprived The Hague of any significant support in the UN. Sukarno's Indonesia was a leading voice in the emerging Non-Aligned Movement and it could rely on considerable Afro-Asian backing for its claims. Although the United States and its allies were wary of the Jakarta regime and its close relations with Moscow, they did not relish a confrontation in which the Netherlands, a NATO member, could be portrayed as an intransigent imperialist pitched against Indonesia's 'decolonizing' mission. Taking the obvious message from this diplomatic situation – and harried by Indonesian commando attacks in the territory – the Dutch negotiated a withdrawal agreement in 1962 [131].

In the international circumstances of the time the United Nations was the obvious body to manage the implementation of this agreement. The resulting UN operation had two components. The first was the familiar one of military observation. A mission was assembled to supervise the disengagement of Dutch security forces and the Indonesian commandos who had infiltrated the territory. The second part of the UN undertaking was more novel and ambitious. The United Nations Temporary Executive Authority (UNTEA) took over the government of the territory from the Dutch as an intermediate stage in the transfer of power to Indonesia. It was, moreover, a UN government with its own army, the United Nations Security Force (UNSF). While the observers were drawn from the increasingly familiar list of middle powers, the main body of the Security Force was provided by one state, Pakistan. Established in October 1962, the operation was completed by May of the following year when Indonesia took over the administration of the territory from UNTEA. Judged against its mandate the enterprise was wholly successful. The two-stage transfer of power took place in a secure and tranquil atmosphere. The Dutch were spared the humiliation of transferring power directly to their enemy. More broadly, the issue remained insulated from cold war politics. The wider morality of the affair was altogether muddier, however. The UN was instrumental in delivering a largely reluctant people to the undemocratic rule of an alien and distant capital. An 'act of self-determination' to be administered by Indonesia as part of the settlement was, as widely expected, a mere sham when it took place in 1969. The operation in West New Guinea was a corrective to the view that the UN's peacekeeping ventures would always occupy a moral high ground above considerations of *realpolitik*. The outcome of the operation may have served the larger purpose of cold war management. It had, though, little to do with democracy and self-determination [84; 159].

The two succeeding UN interventions were more modest military observer missions. The first of these was in the Arabian peninsula. In 1963–64 the United Nations Yemen Observation Mission (UNYOM) supervised the withdrawal of Saudi Arabian and Egyptian forces from opposite sides in the civil war then underway in Yemen. Then in 1965 and 1966 another military observer mission was deployed between India and Pakistan to supervise the disengagement of forces following the outbreak of large-scale fighting. This United Nations India–Pakistan Observation Mission (UNIPOM) operated in parallel with the earlier UNMOGIP which continued its work in Kashmir. UNIPOM's operations were centred on another sensitive area of the border, that between what was then West Pakistan (later the new state of Bangladesh) and northern India. In both Yemen and the India–Pakistan border the UN was, once again, intervening in crises that were removed from the centre of cold war competition but still liable to be drawn into it if left unattended. In Yemen the royalist, Saudi-backed side was implicitly pro-western, while the republican rebels backed by Egypt were potentially pro-Soviet. In south Asia the alignments were less obviously discernible but still present. Diplomatically, Pakistan tended towards the western bloc while the more robustly non-aligned India had recently developed a certain political *tendresse* towards the Soviet Union [20; 126; 159].

The UN's next major engagement was to be of much greater duration than anything else undertaken during the 1960s. Although unforeseen at the time of its establishment, the UN's peacekeeping commitment in Cyprus would continue through cold war, détente, cold war again and then into the post-cold war world order. The Security Council established the United Nations Force in Cyprus (UNFICYP) in March 1964 after the outbreak of fighting between the island's Greek and Turkish communities. The immediate cause of the conflict was an attempt in late 1963 on the part of the Greek Cypriot president, Archbishop Makarios, to adjust the state's constitution in a way that would reduce the influence of the Turkish Cypriot minority. The constitution, part of the 1960 agreement leading to Cyprus's independence from Britain, had been carefully constructed to safeguard the rights of the minority. The Turkish Cypriot community had been unenthusiastic about the independence that the Greek Cypriots had pursued with considerable violence for a number of years. The constitution had been designed to maintain the integrity of the state against two contending challenges. One of these was the union with Greece (*enosis*) aspired to by the more militant Greek Cypriots. The other was the partition of Cyprus into two ethnically based statelets, which was favoured by the Turkish community. So delicately balanced between the interests of the two communities was the political structure that had been imposed by the 1960 agreement, and so intense their suspicion of each other, that any interference with basic constitutional provisions was bound to lead to inter-communal conflict [29; 153].

Initially, Britain (which along with Greece and Turkey was a 'guarantor power' of the constitution) took the lead in restoring order by deploying forces that it maintained on the island under the independence agreement. This was not a sustainable position for the former colonial power, however, and London sought to widen the responsibility by internationalizing it. Attention turned first of all to the possibility of a NATO force [158 *p. 82*]. This appeared to make sense as all three guarantor powers were members of the alliance. Cyprus, however, was not in NATO. It was, in fact, a prominent member of the Non-Aligned Movement. Additionally, its Greek Cypriot dominated government was suspicious of what it saw as an American and British preference for the Turkish community. The wider internationalization of the situation through United Nations involvement, the UN having a rapidly growing Non-Aligned membership at this high tide of decolonization, was much more attractive to Makarios. In consequence the Cyprus problem was passed to the Security Council in February 1964 and UNFICYP created the following month. The Soviet Union, which with France was unenthusiastic about this latest extension of the peacekeeping project, abstained on the enabling resolution. The Cyprus crisis was, after all, essentially a domestic problem. Such international implications as it had were largely internal to the western alliance. There were no obvious cold war considerations – beyond the rather negative one for the Soviet Union of maintaining NATO's internal cohesion. Non-aligned Cyprus's own desire for the force, however, ruled out a Soviet veto. But the absence of full Security

Council consensus pointed to a difficult future for the management of the undertaking. Specifically, the continuing dispute over the financial basis of peacekeeping would soon grow into a major crisis for the organization.

In the meantime, secretary-general U Thant faced immediate problems in putting the force together. In a departure from Hammarskjöld's original scheme for middle-power peacekeeping, a permanent member of the Security Council was to make a considerable operational contribution. Britain continued to deploy its forces in the peacekeeping duties it had assumed when the crisis blew up, but now under the UN flag. Other contributors though were not so readily forthcoming. The experience of the Congo had made governments wary of committing forces for UN duty and, at least at the outset, the Cyprus problem appeared to threaten considerable physical risks for the peacekeepers [*Doc. 15*]. Eventually, a group of middle powers – Canada, Denmark, Finland, Ireland and Sweden – was prevailed upon to contribute forces. Moreover, in the uncertain financial circumstances of the operation the contributing states agreed to pay for their own involvement pending reimbursement from the UN in the future. Apprehensions about the dangers likely to be faced by the peacekeepers in Cyprus soon proved unfounded. UNFICYP quickly adopted the now standard interpositionary role between the two communities, each of which accepted its neutrality and moral authority. It soon became clear, however, that the commitment was likely to be a long-term one as the parallel process of peacemaking by successive UN special representatives failed to make significant headway. During the first ten years of the operation periodic outbreaks of violence (most notably at the end of 1967) were dealt with pragmatically by UNFICYP. While unable to resolve underlying conflicts, the peacekeepers were reasonably effective at containing their worst consequences [19; 120; 125].

This situation, largely static for a decade, was dramatically transformed in July 1974. A coup was attempted in confused circumstances by Greek Cypriot extremists against their own government. The aim was *enosis* with the right-wing military regime then in power in Athens (though close to collapse at that time). In response Turkey, whose current government was also markedly nationalistic, launched a major invasion of the island. Initially occupying a relatively small part of the predominantly Turkish area of northern Cyprus, the invaders resumed their advance in mid-August after a short pause. The result was the effective partition of the island and the displacement of about 200,000 Greek Cypriot refugees southwards. Clearly, the capacity of a lightly armed peacekeeping force to intervene decisively in such a military onslaught was limited. The mere physical presence of UNFICYP was, though, probably instrumental in preventing the Turkish force from occupying the Cypriot capital, Nicosia. The international consequences of engaging UN peacekeepers were evidently too great for Ankara to contemplate. This was one small vindication for the principle of moral presence underlying peacekeeping in an otherwise lamentable outcome for UN military involvement [132; 158].

The 'fact on the ground' created by the invasion was the so-called 'Turkish Republic of Northern Cyprus'. This political entity failed to win diplomatic recognition by any state other than Turkey itself. It nevertheless acquired an air of political permanence as peacemaking efforts failed to make any significant progress throughout the rest of the 1970s and the 1980s. In the early post-cold war optimism about a 'new international order', the United States appeared prepared to pursue a permanent solution to the Cyprus problem but it did not survive early set-backs of the type the UN had been doggedly confronting since 1964. There was, in truth, no real American national interest involved to sustain its peacemaking efforts. The passing of the cold war drained the situation of much of its importance for the west as concerns over alliance cohesion became much less urgent. In this sense UNFICYP illustrates a general risk for peacekeeping operations established in areas where even peripheral mutual superpower interests are absent. A lack of impetus towards overall settlement on the part of the big powers meant that the peacekeeping operation became more or less permanent and 'institutionalized'. In this environment peacekeeping could evolve into part of the problem rather than a tool for its solution. The interposition of the UN between the two *de facto* Cypriot states and the local stability this ensured ultimately served the post-1974 political *status quo* rather than the building of a consensus for a mutually acceptable long-term settlement.

FINANCE AND AUTHORIZATION: THE ARTICLE 19 CRISIS

While UNFICYP pursued its peacekeeping objectives on the ground, the Cyprus operation was at the centre of a major institutional crisis in New York. Divisions within the Security Council on the question of the financing of peacekeeping had, as we have seen, been present since the time of Suez. Underlying this, however, was the more fundamental political issue of the authorization and control of operations. It was, in short, about power, prerogatives and interpretations of the

Charter. Its roots could be traced back to the Soviet preoccupation during the planning of the UN in 1945 with the asymmetrical balance of power between east and west in the organization. We have seen how Moscow insisted from the beginning on the primacy of the Security Council – where it could exercise a veto on decisions – over that of the General Assembly where, in the early days of the organization at least, it would almost certainly be out-voted. Peacekeeping, because it was unforeseen by the founders of the organization, had no clear identity in the Charter and so no agreed structures of authorization. Its financing thus became a battlefield in the war between the super-powers over the location of power in the United Nations. Prior to Suez the costs for UNTSO had been covered, without controversy, from the UN's ordinary budget as a 'regular expense' of the organiza-tion. Similarly, the cost of UNOGIL in Lebanon was met from the UN's normal assessments on all members states. Hammarskjöld him-self, it will be recalled, had taken the position in his Summary Study of the lessons of UNEF that the costs of all peacekeeping operations should be considered regular expenses of the UN and should therefore be payable by the whole membership. Initially, the Soviet objection to the financing of UNEF on this basis was not in itself a major problem. Voluntary contributions from the United States and Britain meant that the operation, which was in any case relatively inexpensive, was maintained without forcing any challenge to the Soviet position. While UNEF cost about $20 million annually in the early 1960s, however, ONUC devoured $120 million in 1962 alone [95; 120; 143].

Part of the financial crisis that emerged with ONUC and came to a head over UNFICYP lay simply in the inability of many of the new, less developed members to meet their assessed commitments. But the main factor was the refusal of key states to pay up and the impossibility of others covering these defaults by additional contributions as had happened over Suez. The grounds of the Soviet objection to compul-sory payments for UNEF – its establishment by the General Assembly rather than the Security Council – did not apply to ONUC, which was authorized by Security Council resolution. Moscow, however, rejected the right of the General Assembly to apportion costs as it had been doing under Article 17(2) of the Charter [*Doc. 3(iv)*]. Instead, it insisted, this responsibility lay with the Security Council under Article 48(1) [*Doc. 3.(i)*]. The Soviets took the same rhetorical position that they had over Suez: the cost of the operation should be met by the 'imperialists' who had necessitated its creation (Belgium in the case of the Congo). In addition to this, the Soviet Union argued that despite having been authorized by the Security Council, ONUC had been left far too much to the personal control of the secretary-general. This view was obviously influenced by the conflicts surrounding the conduct and objectives of ONUC in 1960 and 1961. In this way concern over constitutional principle and the creation of undesirable precedents was combined with resentment at the damage being done to actual Soviet foreign policy interests. To drive the point home Moscow began to withhold its assessed contributions to UNTSO in Palestine as well as to ONUC. The Soviet Union was not alone in its rejection of funding by compulsory assessment. Its views were shared by France [84 *p. 446*]. The French position also derived in part from resentment over the course of the UN operation in the Congo. While Moscow denounced ONUC over the fall and death of Lumumba, Paris, from the opposite political bank, objected to the UN's threats to Katangese secession. But the French too had objections in principle to compulsory support for peacekeeping. Under the nationalistic presidency of Charles de Gaulle, France sought to constrain the basic idea of multilateral military intervention. In the French view power in the international system should be distributed among sovereign states alone. The 'power' of the UN ought, therefore, to extend no further than the tasks delegated to it by states in pursuit of their own interests. For the UN to require members to pay for its military operations ran directly counter to this world-view.

By 1961 the financial situation was already chaotic. Defaults in members' payments had caused a shortfall of 40 per cent in ONUC's 1960 budget. In December 1961 the General Assembly voted, over strong Soviet objections, to refer the issue to the International Court of Justice (ICJ) for a judgment on the legal position. The question put for adjudication was whether peacekeeping costs should be imposed by the General Assembly as 'expenses of the Organization' under Article 17(2). Or, were such costs 'extra-ordinary' expenses and as such not recoverable on a compulsory basis by the General Assembly? The advisory opinion of the ICJ ('advisory' because the Court was not permitted to make definitive pronouncements on the Charter) was issued the following July. The ICJ backed the western (and Hammar-skjöld's) position that peacekeeping was indeed a regular expense of the UN and therefore apportionable by the General Assembly on all members [*Doc. 16*] [95; 143].

There was little likelihood that this advisory opinion from an international court that was itself biased towards the west in its composition would change Soviet policy. But sleeping dogs were no longer to be left lying. The United States, scenting some cold war points to be scored, now raised the question of sanctions against those with outstanding debts for peacekeeping. Under Article 19 of the Charter members of the General Assembly in default of payments under Article 17 could in certain circumstances be denied voting rights [*Doc. 3(iv)*]. The Soviet Union responded by announcing that any attempt to apply such sanctions against it would lead to its withdrawal from the General Assembly. Once again, peacekeeping which had been conceived as a means of immunizing areas of world politics from cold war involvement was itself threatening to precipitate a crisis of superpower rivalry within the UN. Full-scale confrontation was avoided, however, as each side weighed the political odds of various courses of action. Just as the Soviet Union had quietly walked away from its *troika* proposal in 1960 when it became clear that crucial Afro-Asian opinion in the Assembly was against it, now the United States recognized that it had overestimated the Assembly's indignation at the Soviet position on the finance issue. In order to avoid the crunch towards which the invocation of Article 19 was propelling the Assembly, the membership as a whole colluded during the 1964–65 session in conducting their meetings on a 'discussion-only' basis. In this way any votes and therefore any question of voting rights could be avoided [*Doc. 17*]. While the immediate threat to the organization had been averted in this way, the underlying problem of the financing and authorization of peacekeeping remained, however. The Cyprus operation had now to be conducted on a precarious, hand-to-mouth basis which tested the goodwill and commitment of the contributing states to the limit [19; 84].

4 THE 1970s AND 1980s: FROM COLD WAR TO DÉTENTE TO COLD WAR

THE EMERGENCE OF DÉTENTE

The 'end of the cold war' has come generally to be dated from the collapse of communism in the Soviet Union and eastern Europe in the late 1980s and early 1990s. Yet this perspective obscures an earlier periodization which saw the cold war as supplanted by 'détente' around the late 1960s, which was itself then displaced by a second cold war at the end of the 1970s. The détente that intervened between the two periods of cold war had various roots. It was in part an acknowledgement by the two blocs (particularly in the aftermath of the Cuban missile crisis) of their 'mutually assured destruction' if they permitted their rivalry to slip out of control. In parallel with this, though, there was a growing awareness in the 1960s of the benefits to be derived from some economic and technological interdependency. These developments led to a consensus between the superpowers that international conflicts should, where possible, be mutually resolved rather than unilaterally exploited [27; 36; 37].

This thinking was, of course, very much in line with the original justification of peacekeeping as a means of containing peripheral disputes before they became enmeshed in the larger bipolar contest. Détente thus brought a much closer marriage between superpower perceptions of their own interests and the peacekeeping idea. A fundamental shift in the balance of forces within the UN itself also contributed to a new attitude on the part of the superpowers. Throughout the 1960s membership of the organization had expanded with the admission of ever more newly independent states as the European colonial empires broke up. By the later 1960s the built-in western majority in the General Assembly of the 1940s and 1950s had long gone. Now the national delegations to the Assembly were for the most part non-aligned with a tendency towards an 'anti-imperialism' that was implicitly hostile to the west. The Soviet Union's historical suspicions about the organization had therefore been greatly lessened. However superficial and short-lived détente would eventually prove, the 1970s represented a distinct period in superpower relations and, by extension, the development of UN peacekeeping [25; 84].

THE MIDDLE EAST 1973–1974

The principal area in which 'détente peacekeeping' took place was the Middle East, which had moved relentlessly towards the centre of superpower rivalry in the late 1950s and 1960s. The Soviet Union's backing for the Arab states in their conflict with Israel became increasingly emphatic during these years. Israel in turn had become ever more dependent on the diplomatic and military patronage of the United States. As the region came more and more to preoccupy the superpowers in the 1960s, so the space for UN involvement contracted. No UN operation was mounted in the aftermath of the Six-Day War of 1967 to replace UNEF, which had been withdrawn following removal of host-state consent by Egypt. The war had been a victory for Israel (and by extension western interests) and although the Security Council did call for the withdrawal of Israeli forces from Arab territory occupied in the fighting, no measures, whether of enforcement or peacekeeping, were proposed to secure its compliance [52].

   By the next round of the Middle East conflict in 1973, however, the international environment had changed. Détente now dictated an unprecedented level of superpower co-operation. On 6 October 1973, during the Jewish festival of Yom Kippur (and the Arab one of Ramadan), Egypt, now lead by Nasser's successor, Anwar Sadat, along with Syria launched a surprise attack on Israel. The Egyptians advanced from the west through Sinai, and Syria from the east in the Golan Heights. Initial Arab gains were reversed when the momentum of surprise faded and the formidable Israeli armoured divisions began to push the attacking forces back on both fronts. The United States and the Soviet Union, taken genuinely by surprise, began to supply their respective clients in the region only after an initial period of indecision. Their support in this era of détente was tentative and wary. Their instinct now was to combine in managing the conflict rather than to pursue victory for their rival *protégés* [Docs 18, 19]. To this end, on 19 October the Soviet leader Leonid Brezhnev invited US President Richard Nixon's secretary of state Henry Kissinger to travel immediately to Moscow to work out the basis of a cease-fire

[41 *p. 524*]. This was quickly concluded on 21 October and Israel, Egypt and Syria were effectively 'informed' by the superpowers that they were no longer fighting. The next day a unanimous Security Council resolution confirmed the cease-fire and called for its implementation within twelve hours. With the tide of the war turning in its favour, Israel was initially reluctant to comply and continued its encirclement of the Egyptian Third Army on the western side of the Suez Canal. There was now a momentary crisis in superpower co-operation when the Soviet Union moved nuclear weapons into the region and the US responded by putting its own nuclear capacity on high alert. This flash-back to pre-détente cold war conditions seemed to concentrate minds, however and Israel now fell into line [5; 13; 30].

The second United Nations Emergency Force (UNEF II) was the first peacekeeping operation to be established since UNFICYP in 1964. Authorized by the Security Council on 25 October, it was quickly deployed between the Egyptian and Israeli lines in Sinai. It was in all meaningful respects an American-Soviet initiative. The key players in its creation were Kissinger and the Soviet foreign minister, Andrei Gromyko. The role of the UN secretary-general, at this time the Austrian Kurt Waldheim, who had succeeded U Thant in 1971, was in a real sense merely a secondary one. The entire process, from the first Soviet move to the authorization of an interpositionary peacekeeping force, had taken less than a week. The significance of this could be interpreted in different ways, depending on the perspective of the observer. It could be seen as a leap forward for the UN and an illustration of what it could achieve in the absence of superpower rivalry. Alternatively it could be taken as a depressing sign of the subordination of the world organization to superpower interests. In the view of one writer of the more pessimistic perspective, 'the United Nations in general and the Security Council in particular were pushed further along the road to the point where they became mere elements – however essential – in superpower strategy' [158 *p. 106*].

UNEF II was initially formed by elements of UNFICYP hurriedly brought across the Mediterranean from Cyprus. It eventually grew to a strength of 7,000. Its authorizing resolution, making explicit what was now implicit in peacekeeping practice, excluded the participation of the permanent members of the Security Council. The composition of the force did depart in one key respect from the norm of contingents from familiar middle-power activists. For the first time a Warsaw Pact state (Poland) contributed troops to a UN peacekeeping operation. A further symptom of the impact of détente followed shortly after with the incorporation of Soviet officers in UNTSO to balance exactly the number of their American counterparts. And there was to be no major conflict over the financing of UNEF II. The supremacy of the Security Council (or at least its two key members) in the establishment and control of the force meant that the Soviet Union accepted that costs could be levied on all UN members. Unsurprisingly, given this mutual superpower interest in the force, its deployment and operation were efficient and effective. Both Egypt and Israel (with more reservations) had little option but to co-operate with an intervention which, although having the imprimatur of the United Nations, was in many respects a special project of their respective international patrons [27; 29; 60].

Multilateral involvement on Israel's other front in the 1973 war, that with Syria on the Golan Heights, was not so easily brought about. Although Syrian forces had regained some of the territory lost to Israel in the 1967 war in the first shock of the 1973 fighting, they were eventually pushed back beyond even the previous line. Initially, therefore, the regime of President Hafiz al-Assad in Damascus was not readily receptive to United Nations intervention as it feared a consolidation of the new Israeli gains. Sporadic fighting, mainly in the form of artillery duels, continued across the opposing lines in the Golan Heights for several months after the cease-fire. Kissinger, fearing the consequences for US-Soviet relations of continued Syrian alienation, set about a protracted process of shuttle diplomacy between President Assad and the Israeli prime ministers Golda Meir and, from April 1974, Yitzhak Rabin. By the terms of the agreement that emerged in May 1974 Israel was to withdraw more or less to its post-1967 positions and a United Nations Disengagement Observation Force (UNDOF) placed between the two sides. The Security Council, conforming to recent practice, entered the process only after the superpowers themselves had carried through the substantive negotiations. Accordingly, on 31 May, a Security Council resolution was quickly passed authorizing the establishment of the new force. Again, the UN was essentially an executive wing of superpower diplomacy (or, perhaps more correctly, American diplomacy acquiesced to by the Soviet Union). The UN's institutional role in this was to manage the practical implementation of *faits accomplis*.

The unusual designation of UNDOF as an 'observation force' reflected a compromise between different views of the nature of the operation on the parts of Syria and Israel. Syria, concerned that the operation would be located on its territory, sought to minimize the impression of a substantial 'occupation force'. Damascus therefore favoured a military observer mission on the lines of UNTSO or

UNOGIL which would involve no real or symbolic challenge to its territorial sovereignty. Israel, on the other hand, remained sceptical of the depth of Syria's commitment to any long-term agreement. It therefore suspended its usual posture of antipathy to UN peacekeeping operations and sought the interposition of a large and well-equipped force. This, the Israeli government believed, would give the Syrians pause for thought. The possible gains for Syria of a surprise attack in the Golan Heights would have to be seen against the diplomatic consequences of engaging (or, more likely, pushing aside) a major UN presence. UNDOF, therefore, maintained a strength of just over 1,000 – considerably less than Israel would have wished, but much more than Syria had envisaged [13 *pp. 1093–4*]. Slow to be established and hedged around with misgivings when it was, UNDOF turned out to be the longer-lasting of the two post-1973 Middle East operations. This, of course, was no special mark of success in a peacekeeping operation. It was mainly a reflection of the speed and effectiveness of Israel's peacemaking with Egypt which led to the winding up of UNEF II within six years. Certainly, UNDOF had an invaluable part to play in regional stability, especially in its earlier phase when it was responsible for the temporary occupation of territory from which Israel had agreed to withdraw before its return to Syrian sovereignty. But this precarious role of agent between hostile post-belligerents was quite different from the more radical conciliation process in which UNEF II was participating further to the west [114; 158].

UNEF II remained in operation until 1979 when, in a curious way a victim of the success of the process in which it had been involved, its mandate was terminated at the insistence of the Soviet Union. In January 1974, again following a hurried sequence of shuttle diplomacy by Henry Kissinger, a comprehensive disengagement agreement was signed between Israel and Egypt. In contrast to the limited scope of the Israeli-Syrian disengagement that would be agreed the following May, the plan for Suez was far-reaching and pointed the way to a fundamental political settlement. Israeli forces withdrew eastwards across the Canal to a point about twelve miles from the waterway. Egypt re-occupied the territory up to the Canal and six miles beyond on the eastern side. Beyond this was a zone of similar width occupied by the UN, and to the east of this an Israeli-held strip. Both sides accepted limits on the weaponry they could place in their respective zones on either side of the buffer provided by UNEF II. A subsequent phase, agreed later in 1974, widened the UN's area of responsibility and pushed Israeli lines further back to the east. As well as the presence of UNEF II on the ground, the supervision of the agreement was to involve US air force reconnaissance. The process was not without its difficulties from time to time but it was successful in all essentials. There can be little doubt that this was due largely to the close involvement of the superpowers. The principal impetus came from the United States, which was, of course, Israel's *de facto* ally and with which Sadat's Egypt had an ambivalent relationship. But Soviet cooperation, at least in this first phase of the peacemaking process, illustrated its importance to the superpower relationship. This in turn indicated their commitment to ensuring its success [114; 133].

American initiative, Soviet concurrence and UN interposition brought an unprecedented stability to the Egyptian-Israeli interface which deepened over subsequent years. The conditions were created for the negotiation of a comprehensive peace agreement. The external impetus was almost wholly American, however. In 1978, with strong encouragement from the US president Jimmy Carter, a treaty was agreed between Israel and Egypt at Camp David, the American presidential retreat. The signing ceremony, attended by Anwar Sadat and the Israeli prime minister Menachim Begin, took place in March 1979. The continuation of UNEF II into the new phase of peace implementation had been an underlying assumption throughout the Camp David negotiations. The process had, however, been driven by the United States and the UN had no significant input into the final agreement. This simultaneous marginalization of UN authority with exploitation of its peacekeeping resources was a viable policy only so long as both superpowers were pursuing mutual ends. The unilateral 'colonization' of the Egyptian-Israeli rapprochement by the United States meant that this was no longer the case. Soviet acquiescence was withdrawn as the broader diplomatic implications of the agreement began to emerge. The completion of the Camp David process – unthinkable only five years or so earlier – had a major impact on Middle Eastern politics and, inevitably, on superpower relations. By making peace with Israel, Egypt had placed itself beyond the pale of acceptable behaviour in the rest of the Arab states, which rejected the basic notion of a peace agreement with the historic enemy [54; 56].

The Soviet Union now faced a dilemma. Although Moscow was closely associated with the earlier peacekeeping process in Sinai and had accepted the establishment and deployment of UNEF II without demur, it had done so while maintaining its ties with the Arab world as a whole. The isolation of Egypt from this world was now a major diplomatic complication for Moscow. As long as UNEF II served as a traditional interpositionary presence between Egypt and Israel, the superpowers could give their mutual support to it in the spirit of détente and without compromising their existing ties with other regional states. Now, however, the success of US diplomacy in removing the Egyptian-Israeli relationship from the broader Middle East conflict threatened this arrangement. The role of UNEF II, if it was to continue in place, would now change from that of buffer between Arab and Israeli to facilitator of a western-driven, 'anti-Arab' accommodation. This was too great a step for Moscow to take. Détente, as one of its proponents, Henry Kissinger, himself later wrote, 'defined not friendship but a strategy for a relationship between adversaries' [13 p. 600]. The Camp David settlement was in effect a victory for the west, and the Soviet Union now raised its adversarial colours once again. It would not, it made clear, agree to the continuation of UNEF II as hand-maiden to Camp David. Dependant as it was on regular Security Council renewals of its mandate, the operation could not be maintained and accordingly UNEF II ceased to exist in July 1979.

In truth the broader fabric of détente was beginning to unravel at this time anyway. The sequence of communist victories throughout Southeast Asia in the later 1970s, as well as new areas of ideological conflict, particularly in Africa, had been steadily exposing its limits. Soviet disaffection over Camp David was both a symptom of the decline of détente and a further cause of that decline. This shift of the superpower relationship back to a less equivocal form of bipolar contest was evidenced elsewhere in the Middle East in the late 1970s where another venture into détente peacekeeping was running into difficulty [30; 36].

LEBANON: DÉTENTE IN DECLINE

Lebanon was first the subject of UN military involvement in 1958, it will be recalled, when UNOGIL provided a sedative presence through a nervy period of domestic and Middle Eastern regional tensions. Despite the successful outcome of that UN intervention, the local instabilities which necessitated it were endemic. Lebanon's apparent prosperity in comparison to its Arab neighbours (it had often been referred to as 'the Switzerland of the Middle East') and the apparent cosmopolitanism of its urban elite camouflaged deep socio-political fissures. Complex and interrelated factors of geographical location, diverse ethnic composition and instability of government meant that the Lebanon's very existence as a state was precarious. Long-standing problems of Muslim–Christian tensions (and indeed intra-Muslim and intra-Christian sectarian conflicts) were exacerbated with the creation of Israel in 1948 and the sequence of Arab-Israeli wars which

followed over the next quarter century. Lebanon became a major des-
tination for Palestinian refugees both directly from their dispossessed
homes and, in 1970, from Jordan when it expelled its own population
of Palestinian exiles. By the mid-1970s much of the southern part of
Lebanon as well as areas of the capital, Beirut, were occupied by
Palestinians, who now made up about 20 per cent of the country's
population. Concentrated in semi-permanent camps with few amenities
but no shortage of arms, the obedience of this Palestinian population
to the central government in Beirut was minimal. Its loyalty was primarily to the Palestine Liberation Organization (PLO), at this time
the main armed opposition to Israel in the Middle East and throughout the world. With southern Lebanon constituting the border with
northern Israel this was obviously an extremely worrying situation for
Tel Aviv [29; 158].

In 1975 a long-threatened civil war broke out between rightist
Maronite Christian Militias and an alliance of Palestinians and left-
wing Lebanese Muslims. The rickety foundations of the Lebanese
state and the inherent weakness of central authority were quickly
exposed. In the absence of any internal force of stabilization, a
dangerous international situation soon developed. To the south, Israel
was naturally sympathetic to the anti-Palestinian Christians, while to
the east Syria was faced by a political and strategic dilemma. Although
the natural sympathies of Damascus lay with the Palestinian-Muslim
alliance, it had a prior concern with regional stability. The consequences for this of the collapse of the Lebanese state and its replacement by aggressive and well-armed competing factions would be
grave. It would be an obvious provocation to Israel for Syria to
invade and impose its own pro-Muslim solution throughout Lebanon.
The Syrians therefore intervened in 1976 not in support of the
Palestinians but to prop up the Christian-dominated regime in Beirut.
Israel, for its part, accepted this involvement on condition that the
Syrians did not press too close to the Israeli border in the south. The
effect of this was to keep the forces of a long-standing enemy away
from Israeli territory, certainly. But it also meant that the Palestinian-
dominated south remained unconstrained by the Syrian presence,
which was restricted to the north. Cross-border attacks on Israel from
southern Lebanon therefore increased in frequency and destructive-
ness until, in March 1978, the Israeli army moved across the border
in force [60; 133].

With the continuing Egyptian-Israeli peace negotiations moving
towards a conclusion, the United States was determined to stabilize
the situation in southern Lebanon before it could threaten the process. Its

shock-waves could not be allowed to undermine the delicate architecture of diplomacy leading towards Camp David. As in 1973 Washington procured a solution to its diplomatic difficulties through a UN peacekeeping operation. Now, however, with Moscow disaffected from the peacemaking effort between Tel Aviv and Cairo, and with détente as a whole under increasing stress, the Soviet Union could not be co-opted into the process with the ease it had been five years earlier. The operation in Lebanon was established in the twilight of détente and its fortunes would reflect this ambiguous beginning. The United Nations Interim Force in Lebanon (UNIFIL) was authorized by the Security Council during a sequence of meetings on 19 March 1978, when the Soviet Union abstained on the enabling resolutions, though it did not veto them [*Doc. 20*]. UNIFIL was mandated to oversee an Israeli withdrawal from southern Lebanon and itself to fill the territorial and security vacuum thus created. It was also to help the Beirut government to regain its authority in the area. As this 'authority' had been difficult to discern even before the Israeli invasion, however, it was difficult to see how UNIFIL should proceed with this. Assailed in the Security Council by Soviet objections, the Americans were also faced with Israeli grievances. Tel Aviv, after its uncharacteristic support for the interposition of a UN force in the Golan Heights in 1974, now reverted to its more familiar stance of sullen acceptance. Washington, Israel felt, should have shown more understanding of its difficulties over Lebanon before imposing a UN intervention on it.

The absence of outright Soviet opposition meant that controversy was avoided over the operation's financing. But while the principle of General Assembly apportionment as a regular expense was accepted, the reality was that the Soviet Union initially and later the United States too were slow to pay up [133 *p. 341*]. The recognition of mutual self-interest that had earlier driven arrangements over Sinai and the Golan Heights was gone. The international setting of the operation had greater similarities to the Cyprus force than to UNEF II or UNDOF. UNIFIL was seen by the Soviet Union as a western response to a problem of western international relations – those between the United States and Israel – just as UNFICYP sought to resolve the western problem of intra-NATO strains between Greece and Turkey. Superpower differences were also reflected in the refusal of any Warsaw Pact states to contribute to UNIFIL, thus signalling a retreat from the advances of 1973 in UNEF II and UNTSO. There were, though, enough offers of participation to ensure the formation of the force. As usual the majority of contributors were from the traditional middle powers, with contingents sent from Canada,

Finland, Ireland, the Netherlands, Norway and Sweden. France also provided a contingent, however. This French participation was analogous to that of Britain in the Cyprus operation. In both cases there was a particular post-colonial relationship involved. France had been responsible for the administration of Lebanon under a League of Nations mandate after the dismantling of the Ottoman Empire. It had maintained a special relationship after the creation of a Lebanese state during the Second World War. As with Britain in Cyprus, France was somewhat compromised by a traditional affinity with one of the Lebanese factions. But while Britain's historical leaning towards the Turkish community in Cyprus did not significantly affect its standing in the UN force, supposed French sympathy for the Maronite Christians became a problem for UNIFIL. After a series of controversial incidents, the major part of the French contribution was withdrawn in the mid-1980s [42; 158].

UNIFIL was deployed in southern Lebanon in the first days of April and within a month a force of 6,000 (2,000 more than originally planned) was on the ground. Its area of operations should have been all of southern Lebanon from the Israeli border northwards to the Litani River. In reality the actual area of UNIFIL control was cross-cut with enclaves controlled by local factions. Although the Israelis dutifully handed over to UNIFIL the northernmost part of the territory they had occupied, they became less co-operative as they withdrew south. Along the area adjacent to its frontier Israel passed control not to the UN but to local Christian militias. The fearsomely anti-Palestinian stance of these irregular forces provided Israel, in the view of its leaders, with a more reliable buffer (its so-called 'security zone') than any UN peacekeeping force could provide. These local conditions posed a serious challenge to the traditional concept of UN peacekeeping and raised questions about UNIFIL's capacity to carry out the tasks in hand. How appropriate was a lightly armed, interpostionary force in the tortuous international and domestic crosscurrents of southern Lebanon in 1978? How effective was the moral force supposedly deployed by the simple fact of a UN presence in this situation? It is possible that a more strongly armed force mandated to protect Israel's border might have caused Tel Aviv to permit UNIFIL's full deployment and freedom of movement [158 p. 129]. But, of course, such a force would have represented a shift from peacekeeping to enforcement. It would have required contributors to give a freer hand (and heavier weapons) to the UN. But more significantly, it would probably have required a mandate under Chapter VII which would almost certainly have brought a Soviet veto. The Lebanon situation was a sharp illustration of the central dilemma of UN military intervention in the (re-emerging) cold war: the play-off between what would be operationally effective against what was politically feasible.

The difficulties for UNIFIL did not come from the Israeli side alone. The Palestinian forces in southern Lebanon insisted on retaining various positions amidst the UN zone. More substantially, they also insisted on retaining control of the port city of Tyre on the Mediterranean coast south of the Litani river. From the beginning, therefore, UNIFIL did not have full freedom of movement in its own operational area, a fatal weakness for any peacekeeping operation well-recognized since the Congo. From the beginning, therefore, UNIFIL's operations were hampered by a fundamental strategic shortcoming and by tactical disabilities. A lack of effective superpower backing for the UN's efforts was aggravated by restricted mobility and limited firepower. With these handicaps taken into consideration, however, UNIFIL was in many respects successful during its first years of deployment. It provided a buffer, if not directly between Israel and its enemies, then certainly between pro-Israeli and anti-Israeli factions in Lebanon. It could not, though, impose a peace on this cockpit of regional tensions, and four years after UNIFIL's deployment it was effectively brushed aside as the principal players re-entered the arena [152; 154].

The Israeli invasion of June 1982, which reached to the southern outskirts of Beirut, was provoked by an increase in attacks across the border which neither UNIFIL nor the Christian militias seemed capable of preventing. Israel was now determined to settle the 'Palestinian problem' in Lebanon once and for all. In this it was largely successful, though at a considerable cost in national prestige. The PLO was now effectively expelled from Lebanon. This had been achieved, however, with much apparently indiscriminate violence on the part of Israel. Artillery attacks on Palestinian areas of West Beirut and Israeli complicity in factional atrocities – which the UN proved incapable of preventing – pushed Tel Aviv's already declining standing in western public opinion lower still. For the three years following Israel's second invasion of Lebanon in 1982 UNIFIL's *raison d'être* was unclear. It could perform no significant peacekeeping function, interposition being meaningless in an area now dominated by the Israeli occupiers and their local allies. Nevertheless, every six months the Security Council voted to renew its mandate with a view to the eventual resumption of its peacekeeping role [133].

When the Israelis withdrew once again in 1985 they left behind an expanded security zone which further restricted UNIFIL's authority.

In one respect, though, its general position was improved. As the cold war succumbed to another, this time final, thaw with the Gorbachev ascendancy in Moscow, the Soviet Union abandoned its policy of abstention on UNIFIL votes. Henceforward the operation would have the unanimous support of the permanent members of the Security Council. This did not, however, bring any obvious change in its position on the ground. It remained vulnerable to physical attack and political recrimination from the tangle of factions it was forced to confront. It did, however, have a humanitarian role, often in the wake of violent outbreaks it was unable to prevent. It also provided an international 'witness' to events in the region and was therefore something of a constraint on the behaviour of the protagonists. This role was in evidence in 1996 when the Israelis launched intensive air attacks against their Islamist enemies, the Hezbollah, in 1996. (This more fundamentalist Muslim opposition had replaced that of the PLO after the latter's expulsion.) As with peacekeeping operations generally, the pertinent question over UNIFIL was perhaps not what it had 'done' in a positive sense but rather what would have happened in its absence.

PEACEKEEPING IN THE SECOND COLD WAR

For ten years after the formation of UNIFIL no new peacekeeping force or military observer mission was authorized by the UN. The Lebanon operation was perched on the cusp of the shift from détente peacekeeping to the effective suspension of new military interventions by the UN. Conceived in the dying days of détente, UNIFIL was required to operate throughout the ensuing resumption of hostilities between Washington and Moscow. The aggressive instincts of local clients would no longer be suppressed by the two superpowers for the greater good of their own bilateral relationship. Although there were no new UN operations for a decade after 1978, this did not mean that 'international peacekeeping' as a whole went into suspension. Multilateral operations were still mounted, but in both purpose and composition they were now sectional undertakings. These new forces were for the most part substitutes for (or extensions of) operations previously undertaken by the UN.

As we have seen, Soviet alienation from the US-driven peace process between Egypt and Israel led to the winding up of UNEF II in 1979, even though a peacekeeping role remained to be performed during the implementation of the Camp David agreement. Consequently, and with some reluctance, the Americans became responsible for the creation of a non-UN replacement for UNEF II. In 1981 agreement was reached between the United States, Israel and Egypt for the creation of the 2,500-strong Multinational Force and Observers (MFO). Lacking the clear identity of a UN operation, however, the MFO faced a number of structural problems at its deployment in 1983. Despite – or perhaps more correctly because of – its essentially western character, it proved difficult to gather an appropriate range of contributors and to retain them. Wariness was felt among European participants at involvement in what was widely perceived as an American foreign policy project [133 *pp. 125–30*]. But given the nature of its task – the supervision of a carefully negotiated and fully-agreed peace treaty guaranteed by the United States – the MFO faced no great operational challenges.

The same could not be said of another western-inspired venture which was designed as an alternative to wider UN involvement in Lebanon. When, following its 1982 invasion, Israel set about the expulsion of the Palestinians from their strongholds in West Beirut, there was an obvious danger of a clash with the Syrian forces deployed in the area since the intervention in 1976. An extension of UNIFIL's mandate and its interposition between the two sides would have been one means of easing the situation. But with the crumbling of détente, Soviet support for UNIFIL, never enthusiastic, was now non-existent. On the other side, the United States was now more reluctant than during the era of détente to confront Israeli objections to the UN role in Lebanon. Instead a western peacekeeping operation was mounted by 2,000 American, French and Italian troops. This Multinational Force (MNF), which was created in August 1982, contributed to the largely incident-free removal of about 7,500 Palestinian fighters from West Beirut and prevented the escalation of tension between Israeli and Syrian forces.

Had the west now wound up the operation it would have been recorded as a small but significant victory for non-UN peacekeeping. But buoyed by this limited success, a longer-term presence for the force was agreed. With its strength doubled to about 4000 (now including a small British contingent), the operation was re-designated as MNF II. The purpose of the operation now was to bolster the authority of the weak and demoralized Lebanese army and to act as an interpositionary force between the Israelis and the local Muslim militias which remained after the departure of the Palestinians. Such interposition, however, could only work if the neutrality and legiti-macy of the buffer forces were accepted on both sides. Without the obvious legitimization of a UN mandate this would always be a problem in the fractured circumstances of Lebanon. Here, though, the obviously sectional composition of MNF II made the situation especially difficult. The force was inevitably characterized by the militias as an instrument of pro-Israeli western 'imperialism'. Throughout 1983 the situation in Beirut deteriorated. Increasingly, MNF II found itself in 'conventional' armed conflict with the militias and therefore departing ever further from a peacekeeping role properly defined. In October 1983 co-ordinated suicide bomb attacks against the force killed over 300 American and French troops. The operation was quickly wound up and the situation in Beirut thereafter continued its downward spiral unhindered by peacekeeping efforts on the part of the UN or anyone else [29; 133].

In the 1950s and 1960s peacekeeping had provided the UN with a means of sealing off superpower involvement in local conflicts peripheral to their main interests. In the 1970s, when cold war gave way to détente, it had offered the superpowers themselves a tool for the management of relationships between troublesome clients. Now, in the 1980s, with bipolar competition sharpened once again and the second cold war under way, no third phase of UN peacekeeping emerged to meet the new situation.

5 A 'NEW MULTILATERALISM'? PEACEKEEPING AFTER THE COLD WAR

THE END OF THE COLD WAR: PEACEKEEPING UNSHACKLED?

The long period of dormancy in UN peacekeeping that followed the creation of UNIFIL was succeeded by a veritable explosion of new commitments as bipolarity began to dissolve in the late 1980s. The next decade – up to the beginning of 1998 – saw about twenty new peacekeeping and military observer missions of significant size as well as a cluster of smaller ones established across the world. Even in the period up to UNIFIL in 1978 from the formation of the UN in 1945, only fifteen operations had been established, and three of those involved an observer corps of less than 100. Five of these earlier commitments (UNTSO, UNMOGIP, UNFICYP, UNDOF and UNIFIL) remained active, swelling even further the plethora of commitments in the late 1980s and 1990s. The extent and distribution of the new operations reflected not just the effect of the end of the cold war on relationships inside the Security Council, but also the altered geography of conflict which came with it. Six of the larger of these new commitments were in Europe (five in various parts of the former Yugoslavia and one in Georgia). Two were in a new area of Middle East tension: the borders of Iraq. Of the others eight were in Africa, three in Central America and the Caribbean, and one in Cambodia.

Inevitably, this new peacekeeping activity generated much optimism about a 'new world order' in which multilateral intervention would become the primary recourse in international conflicts. There was an assumption that the political and security 'no-go areas' of the cold war were now opened up to UN involvement and that their problems, intractable so long as they were at the point of superpower rivalry, would now virtually solve themselves with modest encouragement from the UN. Moreover, the new peacekeeping would not only be unconstrained by superpower rivalry, it could be strengthened by the active participation of the superpowers at the operational level as the political rationale preventing this no longer applied. If there was now no superpower competition then there was no reason to exclude superpower participation. Certainly, there were early signs that the prospects for future UN peacekeeping could be bright. In the period up until the fall of Gorbachev and the disintegration of the Soviet Union at the end of 1991, the superpowers appeared to be trying to outdo each other in their public commitment to a new multilateralism. Moscow, suddenly in search of a post-cold war international identity, appeared to toy for a time with the idea of assuming the part of activist middle power. The UN offered an obvious stage for the performance of this role of international good citizen. A new international status might thus be rescued by Moscow from the debris of its defeat in the cold war. To this end a large part of the Soviet peacekeeping debts (the accumulation of unpaid assessments going back to the 1960s and which amounted to some US$200 million in the late 1980s) was paid off. In response the United States could do little but commit itself to the payment of its own peacekeeping assessments which it had with-held since the mid-1980s during the strongly anti-UN period of its foreign policy under President Reagan [140; 146; 157].

True to the perception of a new peacekeeping untrammelled by superpower rivalries, the first operations of the post-cold war period were successfully undertaken in areas which would previously have been regarded as 'inappropriate' for multilateral intervention. During 1988, for example, a small Good Offices Mission in Afghanistan and Pakistan (UNGOMAP) was established to assist in the process of Soviet withdrawal from Afghanistan. As the Soviet invasion of that country in 1979 had been a major factor in the crumbling of détente and the return to cold war, UN involvement suggested the passing of the core interests from which the superpowers had hitherto excluded all third-party intervention.

POST-COLD WAR PEACEKEEPING IN ASIA AND AFRICA

This impression was reinforced the following year with the creation of the first Angola Verification Mission (UNAVEM I). The purpose of this was to supervise the withdrawal of the Cuban forces that had been in Angola since the time of its independence from Portugal in 1975 and which had assisted the pro-Soviet government against both South African incursions and western-backed rebels. Thus another cockpit of the second cold war moved into the range of UN peace-keeping [118].

The Cuban withdrawal overseen by UNAVEM I was itself facilitated by a major UN operation undertaken in 1989 and 1990 in Namibia. Namibia (previously South West Africa) had been a major issue in both the Security Council and the General Assembly since the 1960s. Originally a German colony, it had been passed under League of Nations mandate to South Africa after the First World War. This arrangement continued when the UN established the Trusteeship system in 1945. Far from preparing the territory for self-determination and eventual statehood as required by the UN, however, the apartheid regime in South Africa had effectively annexed it. Namibia thus formed the border between South Africa and Angola. Each of the two regimes supported guerrilla groups fighting against the other. South Africa also used Namibia as its base for regular military incursions into Angola. Worn down by international pressure and faced with a growing crisis of military morale, South Africa eventually agreed to Namibia's independence. The United Nations Transition Assistance Group (UNTAG) was formed to administer the process. UNTAG was one of the UN's most ambitious undertakings to date. With about 8,000 personnel (4,500 troops, 1,500 police and 2,000 civilians) its role was similar to (though more formidable than) that of UNTEA/UNSF in West New Guinea in 1962–63. Despite having to navigate phases of considerable tension between the remaining South African forces and their guerrilla enemies who were set to take power on independence, UNTAG was successful in organizing elections and guiding the territory to statehood in March 1990 [144].

This type of commitment was later undertaken, though with less obvious success, in another area of post cold-war tension, Cambodia. In March 1992 the United Nations Transitional Authority in Cambodia (UNTAC) was established to provide a temporary administration for the country pending UN-organized elections. The deployment followed the signing of an agreement in Paris in October 1991 between the internal factions that had been in conflict with each other and with various foreign forces in the country since the mid-1970s. Cambodia's misfortunes during these years had derived from its geographical position. Its proximity to Vietnam inevitably drew it into the maelstrom of ideological and strategic conflicts centred there. UNTAC was a massive undertaking, consisting of some 22,000 military and civilian personnel. Its mandate ended in September 1993 following elections for a new inter-party government. But however effective the UN operation had been in achieving its specific administrative objectives in Cambodia, the longer-range fortunes of the country were not transformed. The country remained dangerously unstable after the winding up of UNTAC [106; 108; 117].

The absence of a clear resolution to Cambodia's fundamental political problems served to illustrate the shortcomings of post-cold war peacekeeping and the fallacy of some of the more optimistic assumptions surrounding it. In a number of key areas the end of the cold war, far from liberating the peacekeeping project, in fact weakened it. Yes, no area was any longer out of bounds to UN peacekeeping. But the reason why peacekeeping was now unconstrained by superpower interests was, axiomatically, that the superpowers no longer *had* any specially strong commitments in these areas. As a result they could no longer restrain the behaviour of client states and opposition movements as they had during the cold war. The assumption, as we have said, was that the removal of the cold war dimension from regional conflicts would automatically resolve them. In reality this exaggerated the importance of the big powers. Many cold war conflicts had been founded in – or had acquired – real local bases. The passing of the cold war did not resolve this, it merely removed the discipline which could once be imposed by strong external influences. The UN, therefore, could be *technically* successful in administering transition in Cambodia, but as the underlying conflicts persisted and as the superpowers no longer exercised themselves in managing them, a fundamental resolution was beyond the capacities of UN peacekeeping.

A similar situation persisted in Angola. UNAVEM I was wholly successful in overseeing the Cuban withdrawal, which was completed ahead of schedule. But this operation had been established to facilitate the high politics of inter-state diplomacy. Angola, Cuba and South Africa, with the background presence of the United States and the Soviet Union, were from the beginning agreed on the process. They required only the formal presence of international observers. But when the UN was enlisted in the search for a final settlement of Angola's civil war between the Marxist MPLA government, historically allied to the Soviet Union, and the UNITA guerrilla movement, which had been sustained by South Africa and the United States, the outcome was much less successful. UNAVEM II, which was established by the Security Council in May 1991, was charged with the management of a peace agreement brokered by the United States and the Soviet Union. Despite this international encouragement towards a settlement and the long history of external interference of which it was a tacit acknowledgement, UNAVEM II was essentially an intervention in the internal politics of Angola. The international dimension of the Angolan crisis had, strictly speaking, been removed with UNAVEM I and the withdrawal of Cuban forces. The conflation of the international and the domestic was not new to the peacekeeping process, but it became a major feature of the post-cold war period and a recurring political and operational problem for the UN [1; 144].

In Angola presidential and parliamentary elections were to be held under UN supervision. Again, the underlying assumption was that with the passing of the cold war its local manifestations would merely wither away. But the Angolan conflict had always had a base in internal ethnic and regional divisions. The effect of years of external encouragement to the warring factions had simply deepened them. The electoral process collapsed in 1992 when the anti-government forces withdrew as their defeat at the polls became evident. The resulting resumption of fighting was more destructive than anything which had preceded it during the cold war. A chastened UN renewed its efforts with the creation of UNAVEM III in 1995, which approached its task with a fuller appreciation of the 'Angolan' character of the conflict and its potential intractability.

The limits of post-cold war peacekeeping were also apparent on the other side of Africa. In Somalia too, between 1992 and 1995, local conflicts not only endured but worsened long after they had ceased to have a place in superpower competition. Additionally, Somalia pointed up the disastrous consequences that could follow direct superpower involvement in UN peacekeeping. Rather than the positive post-cold war developments foreseen by the optimists, American domination of a central phase of UN intervention in Somalia threatened to bring UN peacekeeping as a whole into disrepute. Somalia had been drawn into the second cold war largely because of its strategic location in the Horn of Africa and its extensive coastline on the Indian Ocean. Soviet backing for the revolutionary regime in neighbouring Ethiopia in the 1970s and 1980s brought American support for the Somali regime of Siyad Barre. With the end of the cold war, superpower interest in the region faded. Their respective client governments, both of which were authoritarian, corrupt and deeply unpopular, were now without their powerful patrons and could not sustain themselves. In Somalia the Siyad Barre regime collapsed at the beginning of 1991. Its fall had been the result of the combined pressure of otherwise rival opposition groupings which, their common enemy gone, commenced to confront each other for the spoils. The result was civil war and humanitarian disaster [138; 144].

The UN became involved in the macabre complexities of Somalia only reluctantly after it became clear in early 1992 that a million and a half people, a quarter of the population, were at risk of starvation. The United Nations Operation in Somalia (UNOSOM) was authorized by the Security Council in April 1992 with the objective of securing the delivery of humanitarian aid. Deployment of troops was initially deferred until September, by which time the daily death toll was enormous. The 500-strong Pakistani contingent which spearheaded the operation was immediately faced with the hostility of Mohammed Farah Aydeed, one of the most powerful of the warlords struggling for dominance in the Somali capital Mogadishu. Overwhelmed by the violent and virtually incomprehensible web of local clan and factional politics, UNOSOM proved incapable of protecting aid supplies and ensuring their delivery. International public opinion, formed by a stream of horrifying media images, now pressed for a more decisive intervention. In November the US government offered 30,000 troops for a redoubled UN effort which would, it was hoped, simply overawe the local armed factions. Consequently the Security Council voted in December 1992 to establish a Unified Task Force (UNITAF) under American operational control. A force of 28,000 landed by sea in front of a battery of television cameras before dawn on 9 December 1992.

The mere act of multiplying the number of international troops on the ground did not change the basic situation faced by the UN in Somalia. At the root of the country's ills was the absence of a central authority. From the peacekeeping perspective there was simply no 'host state'. Nor did the domination of the venture by the remaining superpower have any restraining effect. On the contrary, while the post-cold war milieu had opened up peacekeeping to participation by the former bloc leaders, a considerable residue of anti-Americanism remained in the third world. In May 1993 the UN reclaimed the operation by subsuming UNITAF in a second UNOSOM under United Nations rather than United States command, but American forces still predominated in the operation. Fighting between UN forces and the Somali factions, particularly that of Mohammed Aydeed, had led to the death of over 100 peacekeepers by the end of 1994, frequently in gruesome circumstances and with on the spot media coverage. Washington soon lost its initial enthusiasm for the venture and UNOSOM II withdrew from Somalia in March 1995. Its departure was followed immediately and emblematically by a battle between the local warlords for possession of the evacuated UN compound.

The fundamental dilemma for UNOSOM/UNITAF was that in the prevailing circumstances its objectives – the protection and distribution of emergency aid – required an enforcement rather than a peacekeeping operation. In the absence of a consenting state subject to pressure from other states in the international system, and faced by the intense hostility of one of the dominant factions, moral authority and interposition alone could achieve nothing. The UN operation, while frequently taking offensive action, did not fully embrace this enforcement role. It avoided the essential but clearly perilous task of disarming the factions and relied instead on the vain hope that a show of force, both military and diplomatic, would be sufficient to subdue opposition [138; 140].

BOSNIA: PEACEKEEPING AND ENFORCEMENT IN COLLISION

The UN confronted a broadly similar set of circumstances at this time in the former Yugoslavia. Once again the precondition for traditional peacekeeping – a responsive host state – was absent. In Bosnia, however, the United States resisted all pressure to commit its own ground forces to the UN's efforts. Instead the American presence was felt through the parallel involvement of NATO. At the beginning of the crisis in the former Yugoslavia in 1991 there was a widely held view in both Europe and the United States that regional European agencies should undertake any multilateral involvement that might be judged necessary [144 *p. 223*]. The UN itself, now heavily burdened by the explosion of post-cold war interventions elsewhere, was content to go along with this. But as repeated European efforts ran into the quicksand of Balkan politics, it became clear that the UN would be drawn in. In February 1992 the United Nations Protection Force (UNPROFOR) was established. Its mandate to 'create the conditions of peace and security required for the negotiation of an overall settlement of the ... crisis' was based on traditional interpositionary peacekeeping (Security Council resolution 743, 21 February 1992). But in Bosnia, as in Somalia, there was no peace to keep, and UNPROFOR's changing and frequently confused mandate came to reflect this. Although the model for UNPROFOR seemed to be UNFICYP in Cyprus (the UN's other European peacekeeping venture to date), the politico-military conditions were closer to those faced by ONUC in the Congo. The Bosnian crisis, like that in central Africa thirty years before, was about a struggle for territorial and political control of an emergent state by competing ethnic forces. Local 'Muslims', Croats and Serbs were engaged in a three-way fight for control of 'Bosnia' which, following the other components of the former Yugoslavia, found itself impelled towards independence in the early 1990s. As in the Congo, the UN in Bosnia was continually pushed towards the frontier between interposition and enforcement [147].

In August 1992 the Security Council explicitly invoked the enforcement powers of Chapter VII of the Charter in an attempt to establish UNPROFOR's credibility as guarantor of humanitarian aid supplies. But the culture shift from peacekeeping to enforcement proved a difficult one for UNPROFOR to make. Later, in March 1993, the way was prepared for the entry of a more enforcement-orientated agency (and a more local one) when NATO became involved in maintaining a UN-declared no-fly zone. There now began two years of dual UN–NATO military involvement. It was not an easy relationship [119 *p. 80*]. NATO, as a military alliance, consistently took a more robust view of multilateral intervention than UNPROFOR, and refused to assume the role, in the words of its own secretary-general, of 'sub-contractor of the United Nations' [155 *p. 125*]. In particular, differences between the UN and NATO arose over the use of punitive air-strikes against forces (invariably Serb) acting in contravention of Security Council instructions. A so-called 'dual key' was held by the UN and NATO, with each having a veto over action. In practice this seemed to be exercised exclusively by the UN. Tensions in this inter-agency relationship grew after the UN abandoned its declared 'safe area' of Srebrenica to Bosnian Serb forces in August 1995. The ensuing massacres of civilians brought no significant military response from the international agencies involved in the war. Shortly after, the UN was effectively pushed aside when NATO snatched sole control of the dual key and began a sustained air and artillery offensive against the Bosnian Serbs ('Operation Deliberate Force'). This decisive abandonment of the myth of peacekeeping in Bosnia led for the first time in the conflict to meaningful 'peacemaking', which resulted in the Dayton Accord of November 1995 [105; 109].

At the root of this conflict between the UN and NATO lay a clash of two quite distinct institutional – and historical – cultures. The peacekeeping mindset of the UN was personified in Bosnia by the secretary-general's representative, Yasushi Akashi from Japan, who was responsible for the repeated vetoing of NATO proposals for tougher military action. His approach was at odds with the 'war-winning' culture of the latter. NATO was in origin, of course, a cold war military alliance. While it had recently been re-invented as a general regional security agency for the new Europe, NATO was still guided by conventional military doctrine. Tellingly, the international status of the 'non-peacekeeping' Implementation Force (I-FOR) which replaced UNPROFOR after the watershed of Operation Deliberate Force was left unclear. 'Authorized' by the Security Council in December 1995 under Chapter VII, it was effectively controlled by

NATO. Ironically, perhaps, this enforcement operation was conducted in conditions which would have been quite appropriate to traditional peacekeeping. There was now a peace to keep and a clear space for third-party interposition. This had been created, though, by military might.

COLLECTIVE SECURITY REVIVED? OPERATION DESERT STORM

The experience of these UN interventions of the late 1980s and 1990s seems to suggest that peacekeeping was not, after all, liberated by the end of the cold war. On the contrary, it appeared that the passing of bipolarity had actually created new problems for the conduct of peacekeeping. One explanation of this is that, far from being constrained by the cold war, peacekeeping should more correctly be seen as an *artefact* of the cold war. The end of bipolarity meant the end of the international conditions which brought peacekeeping into being. It had emerged in part, it will be recalled, as a means of giving the UN an alternative military role in a system which was structurally incompatible with collective security. But, logically perhaps, there might have been a corollary to this. Could it not be that in a new, non-bipolar global structure the original conception of collective security would come into its own? Events in the Gulf in 1990 and 1991 were seen by many at the time to point in this direction. The response to Iraq's invasion of Kuwait in August 1990 appeared to raise the prospect not of a new dawn for peacekeeping but of a delayed advent for full-blooded international enforcement under Chapter VII of the Charter.

The 'optimistic' view of Operation Desert Storm, as it was known, saw it as a model for genuine collective security in a new world order. The Security Council decided on bold action under Chapter VII and no veto was cast against it. A majority of its permanent members (the United States, Britain and France) then led a military alliance with broad regional and international membership to secure 'United Nations' objectives (Iraq's withdrawal from Kuwait). A more sceptical perspective, however, looked to the example of the Korean campaign rather than the spirit of the Charter for an explanation of Desert Storm. In this view, western foreign policy objectives were pursued by western-led forces with only a tendentious claim to UN legitimization. The Soviet Union had been prevented from using its veto to protect its client (North Korea) in 1950 by the physical absence of its delegation from crucial Security Council meetings. In 1990 it was also prevented from vetoing the undertaking against a client state (Iraq), but this time as a result of its general diplomatic debilitation when the very fabric of Soviet statehood was rending.

The role of the Security Council and the formal basis on which the United States and its allies took action was, in truth, far from clear-cut. A sequence of resolutions following the Iraqi invasion had called for immediate, unconditional withdrawal. Economic sanctions were also applied against Iraq. These resolutions culminated at the end of November with an authorization for member states already co-operating with the (now exiled) government of Kuwait to use 'all necessary means' to implement previous resolutions after a deadline of 15 January 1991 [*Doc. 21*]. Transparently the work of the United States and Britain, Resolution 678 was an invitation to states to sign up to an anti-Iraqi alliance. Yet while this, like previous resolutions, made explicit reference to Chapter VII, it did not amount to a formal call to collective security under the Charter. There was no suggestion that Article 43, which, it will be recalled, requires member states to provide military assistance at the behest of the Security Council, would be invoked. Resolution 678 merely provided the United States with the necessary permission to assemble a force of like-minded powers [144].

This lack of wholesale commitment to the original machinery of collective security as laid out in the Charter was an indication of the limits of the new consensus. The difficulty was not merely one of residual cold war suspicions between east and west. A more profound resistance to multilateralism could be detected. The view persisted that UN member states should pursue their own foreign policy interests in their own ways. States alone must determine how widely or how narrowly to perceive these interests. In short, the fundamental contradiction between sovereignty and collectivity first in evidence in the League of Nations had not been resolved. Bipolarity had, it could be argued, merely provided a false alibi for the deeper flaws of Chapter VII in an international system of independent states. The problems in the concept of collective security, in other words, went much deeper than the specific circumstances of the cold war.

AN AGENDA FOR PEACE

In June 1992, four months after the creation of UNPROFOR and a year after Operation Desert Storm when optimism about developments in UN military operations was still strong, the then UN secretary-general Boutros Boutros-Ghali produced a major report on peace-keeping, *An Agenda for Peace*. This explored the future prospects for peace operations in the wake of a special Security Council summit on the subject held the previous January. The avowed purpose of *An Agenda for Peace* was to reconsider preventive diplomacy, peacekeeping and peacemaking in light of the end of the cold war, what the secretary-general called the collapse of 'the immense ideological barrier that for decades gave rise to distrust and hostility'. *An Agenda for Peace* sought to exploit the momentum of the new interest in peacekeeping. At the same time, however, it showed a fair appreciation of limitations as well as possibilities. The new optimism had, for example, to be conditioned by the fact that some $800 million was still owed to the UN in arrears of members' peacekeeping assessments and that operational commitments for the current year were running at almost $3 billion. But potential new developments were examined and proposals made for reform.

On the central issue of financing, Boutros-Ghali noted that 'a chasm has developed between the tasks entrusted to [the UN] and the financial means provided to it'. He then proposed a number of concrete reforms. These included the creation of a peacekeeping 'reserve fund' to enable operations to be initiated without specific prior financial pledges. He also suggested the building of a 'peace endowment fund' of $1 billion, the interest on which would be used for day-to-day peacekeeping costs. National contributions of peacekeeping forces should also be put on a more formal and reliable basis. Member states should enter long-term agreements with the UN about 'the kind and number of skilled personnel they will be prepared to offer the United Nations as the needs of new operations arise'. This would free the Secretariat from some of the burden of *ad hoc* recruitment from members after an operation had been authorized but before it could be deployed.

On the broader plane, *Agenda for Peace* approached the issue of collective security and the prospects of its being exercised in the new global environment. Forces made available under Chapter VII Article 43 might never, Boutros-Ghali conceded, 'be sufficiently large or well enough equipped to deal with a threat from a major army equipped with sophisticated weapons'. Nevertheless, he urged the Security Council to explore the possibilities of Chapter VII and proposed that the Military Staff Committee should be revived. In the meantime, a new form of military intervention should be considered which would lie between enforcement and peacekeeping. 'Peace enforcement units', formed from volunteers and more heavily armed than peacekeeping operations, could be deployed to implement, by force if necessary, previously agreed cease-fires [*Doc. 22*]. Existing observer and peacekeeping missions had, as we have seen, been insufficient for this purpose in a range of UN interventions in the cold war and after. An encouragement of such half-way-house arrangements between enforcement and peacekeeping was also detectable in the *Agenda*'s revisiting of Chapter VIII of the Charter, which dealt with 'regional arrangements' in the maintenance of peace and security. Although originally envisaged as an adjunct to centralized collective security, the utilization of regional organizations in peacekeeping functions should be encouraged, though concrete proposals to this end were explicitly forsworn by the secretary-general [130; 141].

Challenging though much of *An Agenda for Peace* undoubtedly was, it was ultimately a product of a particular – and essentially transitory – phase in the early post-cold war period. Boutros-Ghali's approach was based on the existence of a new post-bipolar consensus among the big powers. Inherent in this were the assumptions, firstly, that this would continue and, secondly, that the smaller powers would tend to put themselves behind the policies and approaches of the permanent members of the Security Council. In the afterglow of Operation Desert Storm these assumptions may have been understandable, but they inferred a fundamental shift in the nature of international relations on a rather slim historical basis [74 *p. 435*]. As we have seen, Desert Storm was ultimately no more of a genuine UN collective security undertaking than Korea had been. The rapid fragmentation of the anti-Iraq alliance after 1991 and deep divisions among the permanent members of the Security Council on policies to be pursued towards Saddam Hussein's regime in Baghdad in the aftermath of the fighting exposed the fragility of the supposed new consensus.

Little of *An Agenda for Peace* was implemented in any concrete way. No sustained attempt was made to rehabilitate the Military Staff Committee. Article 43 remained dormant. The 'peace enforcement units' as described by Boutros-Ghali seemed tailor-made for subsequent operations in Somalia, Bosnia and Angola, but they did not materialize [157 *p. 94*]. Instead, these crises were subject to various distortions of the traditional peacekeeping model, which usually did not meet the demands of the situations. There were some developments on UN-regional agency co-operation. But the process was not always a happy one, as we have observed over Bosnia. Such interagency relationships tended to be led by the regional organization, with the UN assuming a loose supervisory and legitimizing role in operations initiated elsewhere. This was the case in the 'peacekeeping' operation led by Russia on behalf of the Commonwealth of Independent

States (the former Soviet republics) in Georgia. The UN Observer Mission in Georgia (UNOMIG) established in 1993 exercised a monitoring role over this, but the arrangement was far from the type envisaged by Chapter VIII of the Charter by which regional agencies would be used to implement Security Council decisions. *An Agenda for Peace* marked the high tide of post-cold war optimism and its value lies in the perspective it provides on a particular historical conjuncture. It was significant less perhaps for any tangible changes it precipitated, than for its unintended exposure of the limits of the 'new world order'.

PART THREE: ASSESSMENT

6   THE MULTIPLE PURPOSES OF COLD WAR PEACEKEEPING

To assess the significance of UN peacekeeping in the cold war it is necessary to disentangle its various political purposes. During the cold war the peacekeeping enterprise was important in three more or less distinct areas of political activity: institutional, international and national. Firstly, it had a major role in the politics of the United Nations itself. Secondly, and more obviously, peacekeeping had a part to play in the relationship between the superpowers in both cold war and the interlude of détente. Simultaneously it had an impact on the international relations of the various regions in which it took place. Thirdly, peacekeeping operations were instrumental in shaping the domestic politics of a number of 'host states'. Also at the state level, though perhaps less obviously, peacekeeping was often important in the national politics of the peacekeeper as well as the 'peacekept'.

As an institutional 'device' peacekeeping went some way to rescue the United Nations from military irrelevance. The effect of the cold war on broader global relationships was to cause a clustering in the international state system around the respective ideological poles of the superpowers. This polarization fractured the collectivism necessary for the installation and operation of the security system on which the UN Charter was based. The Korean War merely underlined the futility of pursuing the collective security ideal. Celebrated by the west as a victory for enforcement by the UN, the Unified Command in Korea was simultaneously denounced by the Soviet Union as a western-devised anti-communist crusade. In consequence, by the early 1950s the UN faced an uncertain future as a security organization. With its aspirations to great power unity frustrated, it seemed probable that the UN would slump into one of two equally unattractive futures. It could have declined, *via* platitude and piety, into an anodyne irrelevance in an increasingly dangerous international system. Alternatively, it might simply have become absorbed into the emerging western alliance system. The United States and its supporters dominated the General Assembly, and with the Uniting for Peace resolution in 1950 it was clear that they were willing to use this power to undermine the supremacy of the Security Council. As this supremacy (underscored by the permanent members' power of veto) had been a condition for Moscow's participation in the UN, its subversion could only deepen, perhaps fatally, Soviet alienation. In the event, the expansion and universalization of UN membership which followed the surge of decolonization in the 1960s delivered the UN from these threatened futures. But it would by then have been a much less significant organization if its credibility had not been sustained by an alternative security function in the form of peacekeeping. It would clearly be an exaggeration to say that the peacekeeping enterprise saved the UN from irrelevance or disintegration, but it provided much-needed institutional buoyancy through the most threatening phase of the cold war.

The importance of peacekeeping in the interior politics of the UN was enhanced by its origins in the institution itself. Its early development was determined by the UN rather than any prominent member state or states. The Suez crisis of 1956 gave the *institution* an opportunity to reconceptualize its military function. Partly improvised and partly drawn from the experience of existing military observation missions, the UN Emergency Force was the product of the UN as an organization. The assistance of a group of 'middle powers' like Canada and Sweden in both planning and implementation was obviously essential, but the nature of the project was determined by the institution, and in particular Dag Hammarskjöld, its second secretary-general. This was not, of course, always an unalloyed benefit. The 'leave it to Dag' attitude which followed on the success of UNEF would lead to considerable problems in the Congo. The peacekeeping concept, however impartial in theory, was still vulnerable to political attack in the rigid bipolarity of the 1950s and 1960s. The management of the Congo operation provided the justification for Khrushchev's *troika* proposals in 1960 which challenged one of the fundamental tenets of the UN: the possibility of a disinterested international civil service. Similarly, the wrangles over the financing of peacekeeping – which were at heart about institutional power rather than money – generated another major crisis for the UN over the implementation of Article 19 in 1964. The political 'relevance' that peacekeeping delivered to the UN did not, therefore, come without its institutional price.

These conflicts often appeared to aggravate east–west relations rather than ease them, and in this sense peacekeeping might seem at key points to have been counter-productive. But at least in part the disputes were merely *casus belli*, excuses for a fight, in a fundamentally conflictual relationship. If the grievances over peacekeeping had not existed, others would assuredly have been invented. Overall, the superpower relationship gained from the advent of peacekeeping as the UN worked to seal off local conflicts from their potentially disastrous involvement. How much worse might the discord over the Congo have been if, in the absence of ONUC, the Soviet Union had intervened directly in support of Lumumba and the United States in support of Kasavubu and Mobutu? However bad the situation in the Congo may have been between 1960 and 1964, it never approached the horror in neighbouring Angola in the 1980s where the superpowers simply backed their own local clients and disregarded the UN option. This function of UN peacekeeping in distancing conflicts from superpower involvement reached its apotheosis during the period of détente in the 1970s. The United States and the Soviet Union now seemed to seize control of the UN peacekeeping option from the institution itself in order to exploit it in pursuit of stability in their own relationship. The creation of UNEF II and UNDOF in the aftermath of the 1973 Middle East war, and to a lesser extent the creation of the interim force in Lebanon in 1978, saw the UN acting more or less on the instructions of Washington with Moscow's complicity. Unhappily, the disintegration of détente and reversion to cold war in the 1980s brought an end to this type of peacekeeping but no corresponding return to the earlier cold war form. In fact, the second cold war appeared to mark the end of UN peacekeeping as a palliative in superpower rivalry. The resumption of peacekeeping came only with the end of that rivalry after the conclusion of the cold war itself.

Beyond the bipolar competition, peacekeeping had an obvious role in the management of regional international crises. The Middle East conflict in its various aspects (Egyptian-Israeli; Lebanese-Syrian; Egyptian-Saudi; Syrian-Israeli; Lebanese-Israeli) was a constant object of peacekeeping attention. That the fundamental problems of the region's international relations remained unsolved was a failure of peacemaking not of peacekeeping. The contribution of the various peacekeeping operations in the Middle East cannot be assessed on the basis of positive achievements but only on conjecture about the likely consequences if they had not been mounted. It is an unprovable hypothesis but nevertheless a reasonable one that these consequences would have been very grave at different times and places. The regional stability of other parts of the world was also bolstered by the presence of UN peacekeepers. Again, the basic deficiencies in the relationships between Greece and Turkey over Cyprus and India and Pakistan over their common border were not addressed by the peacekeeping and observer missions. But the regional international relations of the eastern Mediterranean and of south Asia would almost certainly have been the worse for the absence of the UN.

It is at the national level that the success of UN peacekeeping in the cold war becomes problematical. Partly, of course, this is because UN peacekeeping has, strictly speaking, no direct interest in the resolution of national problems. Formally at any rate, states are significant in the peacekeeping process only as sub-systems of the broader international system. It is with the security of the latter that the UN is properly concerned. But the peacekeeping principle of non-interference in national politics has always been more apparent than real. It is beyond any sensible dispute that the United Nations shaped the politics of the Congo in the early 1960s. As it is obviously impossible to construct an alternative history for the Congo had the UN not been involved, we cannot judge whether the three decades of dictatorship, corruption and misgovernment to which the country was subjected after the UN intervention might have been even worse if ONUC had not existed. In West New Guinea the UN operation was complicit in the denial of self-determination to the local population. The subsuming of the Papuan people of the territory into an alien Indonesia which was facilitated by UNTEA/UNSF brought little moral credit to the UN. But, as we have observed, the UN's primary function was the management of international relations. In the circumstances of the early 1960s the outcome of the intervention in New Guinea was probably positive in this respect. The security of the Southeast Asian region was strengthened and the demands of the Afro-Asian bloc in the General Assembly were met. The overall effect of UN intervention in Cyprus is also difficult to assess. UNFICYP carried out a 'model' peacekeeping role with considerable success. It is unclear, though, whether it was actually a positive force in the Cyprus imbroglio over the decades of its operation. Unable to prevent either the Turkish invasion of 1974 or the Greek manoeuvrings which provoked it, UNFICYP may merely have become a part of the problem it was created to manage. In the absence of effective peacemaking, the UN in Cyprus was left to keep (with some success) a peace which was fundamentally unsatisfactory.

The impact of peacekeeping on the national politics of the contributing rather than the host states has been less ambiguous. Ostensibly, participation in peacekeeping operations is about altruism, national sacrifice and international good citizenship. In reality, however, the role of 'peacekeeper' brought advantages to contributing states. For the original middle powers and later the growing number of third world states who took part, contributing forces to the UN conferred a distinct international status. Participation implied stable domestic politics, disciplined and well-trained armed forces, and diplomatic sophistication. Indeed for some states during the cold war – Ireland, India and Sweden among them – UN activism became a central component of foreign policy. Later, smaller less developed states like Nepal and Fiji would acquire an international prestige disproportionate to their tangible national resources through their peacekeeping contributions. At the most practical level too, states could gain from participation. UN service provided operational experience otherwise unavailable to the armed forces of many states. While obviously secondary to the purposes of peacekeeping, this symbiotic distribution of benefits between the undertaking and its participants was an important element in maintaining the supply of peacekeepers apparently in defiance of the normal rules of international behaviour.

Despite the spectacular growth in the number of new operations established from the late 1980s onwards, a great deal of the optimism surrounding the prospects for peacekeeping in the post-cold war world proved misplaced. Much of the 'new world order' thinking which characterized discussion of the UN's role in the 1990s failed to make a distinction between collective security and peacekeeping. Enforcement and interposition were conflated in a loose assumption that UN military intervention of whatever variety was now liberated from the prison of the cold war and would provide the key to a new global security system. In reality there were considerable obstacles to the further development of both collective security and peacekeeping. Like the Unified Command in Korea forty years previously, Operation Desert Storm against Iraq in 1991 could be interpreted as the dawn of 'real' collective security. The truth was that, just like Korea, Desert Storm was a temporary military alliance which had procured a limited legitimization through Security Council resolutions. The passage of these resolutions – in 1950 as in 1990 – was merely a function of the balance of national power in the Security Council at these particular historical points. The central flaw of collective security remained the same as at the time of the League in the 1930s. Sovereign states will always reserve to themselves the power to make decisions about their national interests and will tend to do so according to narrow political and geographical criteria. Cold war bipolarity may have rendered UN collective security unworkable, but only in the sense that a lack of fuel makes a car without an engine unworkable. The larger problem remains under the hood. Peacekeeping was developed to meet those flaws in collective security which derived from the more superficial problem – the empty fuel tank of bipolarity. The forms and practices of peacekeeping were contrived to work round the obstacles of superpower competition. It was, in this sense, a product of the cold war. There was no obvious reason, therefore, why the end of the cold war should enhance its effectiveness. On the contrary, the passing of superpower competition brought a retraction of superpower interests – and the end of their influence over local clients. This moderation of local behaviour by the big powers had been an essential component in cold war peacekeeping from Suez to Lebanon.

The peacekeeping model, with certain modifications, is likely to remain at the centre of multilateral intervention in the absence of an effective system of collective enforcement. It remains the most viable form of international military involvement in local conflicts. Fundamental problems will inevitably remain between the model and the reality. In the real world the division between interposition and enforcement will frequently be unclear; the presence of a peacekeeping force will inevitably impact on local politics; the separation of national crises from international ones will often be impossible. And the passing of the cold war may have brought as many operational drawbacks for peacekeeping as it has institutional improvements. But peacekeeping remains where it was in the cold war: at the conjunction between the best possible and the most desirable.

PART FOUR: DOCUMENTS

DOCUMENT 1   COLLECTIVE SECURITY AND THE LEAGUE
              OF NATIONS

The League of Nations first attempted to introduce a general system of 'collective security' in the aftermath of the First World War. The basic principle remained at the centre of the United Nations' subsequent attempts to regulate international relations. The 'failure' of the League's system was seen by the architects of the UN as due to the limited character of the commitments to be undertaken by member states, particularly in the military field, and the fact that all action had to be agreed unanimously. The Covenant (basic constitution) of the League of Nations outlines the terms of collective security in Articles 10 and 16.

Article 10
The Members of the League undertake to respect and preserve as against external aggression the territorial integrity and existing political independence of all Members of the League. In case of any such aggression or in case of any threat or danger of such aggression, the Council shall advise upon the means by which this obligation shall be fulfilled.

Article 16
1   Should any Member of the League resort to war in disregard of its covenants ... it shall *ipso facto* be deemed to have committed an act of war against all other Members of the League, which hereby undertake immediately to subject it to the severance of all trade or financial relations, the prohibition of all intercourse between their nationals and the nationals of the Covenant-breaking state ...
2   It shall be the duty of the Council in such case to recommend to the several governments concerned what effective military, naval or air force the Members of the League shall severally contribute to the armed forces to be used to protect the covenants of the League
3   The Members of the League agree, further, that they will mutually support

one another in the financial and economic measures which are taken ... in order to minimise the loss and inconvenience resulting ... and they will take the necessary steps to afford passage through their territory to the forces of any Members of the League which are co-operating to protect the covenants of the League.

Covenant of the League of Nations.

DOCUMENT 2   WARTIME POINTERS TO A NEW SECURITY ORGANIZATION

The League became marginal to issues of international security long before the outbreak of the Second World War. But from an early stage in the conflict there was an assumption among the Allied leadership that a new attempt would be made to regulate post-war international relations on a collective basis. In August 1941 the British prime minister Winston Churchill and US president Franklin Roosevelt met aboard ship. The joint declaration which emerged from this – the 'Atlantic Charter' – set out the basic principles for post-war international relations.

[...]

First, their countries seek no aggrandizement, territorial or other;

Second, they desire to see no territorial changes that do not accord with the freely expressed wishes of the people concerned;

Third, they respect the right of all peoples to choose the form of government under which they will live; and they wish to see sovereign rights and self-government restored to those who have been forcibly deprived of them;

[...]

Sixth, after the final destruction of the Nazi tyranny, they hope to see established a peace which will afford to all nations the means of dwelling in safety within their own boundaries, and which will afford assurance that all men in all the lands may live out their lives in freedom from fear and want;

[...]

Eighth, they believe that all of the nations of the world, for realistic as well as spiritual reasons, must come to the abandonment of the use of force. Since no future peace can be maintained if land, sea or air armaments continue to be employed by nations which threaten, or may threaten, aggression outside of their frontiers, they believe, pending the establishment of a wider and permanent system of general security, that the disarmament of such nations is essential. They will likewise aid and encourage all other practicable measures which will lighten for peace-loving peoples the crushing burden of armaments.

US Department of State, *The Foreign Relations of the United States, 1941,* Vol. I (New York: Kraus, 1972), pp. 368–9.

DOCUMENT 3   THE CHARTER OF THE UNITED NATIONS

The Charter is the basic constitution of the United Nations and has the legal force of an international treaty on its signatories (all member states).

(i) *The UN's wide-ranging and legally binding collective security machinery is outlined in Chapter VII, 'Action with Respect to Threats to the Peace, Breaches of the Peace, and Acts of Aggression'. This should be compared with the extracts from the League Covenant in Document 1.*

Article 39
The Security Council shall determine the existence of any threat to the peace, breach of the peace, or act of aggression and shall make recommendations, or decide what measures should be taken in accordance with Articles 41 and 42, to maintain and restore international peace and security.

Article 40
In order to prevent an aggravation of the situation, the Security Council may, before making the recommendations or deciding upon the measures provided for in Article 39, call upon the parties concerned to comply with such provisional measures as it deems necessary or desirable. ... The Security Council shall duly take account of failure to comply with such provisional measures.

Article 41
The Security Council may decide what measures not involving the use of armed force are to be employed to give effect to its decisions, and it may call upon the Members of the United Nations to apply such measures. These may include interruption of economic relations and of rail, sea, air, postal, telegraphic, radio and other means of communication, and the severance of diplomatic relations.

Article 42
Should the Security Council decide that measures provided for in Article 41 would be inadequate or have proved to be inadequate, it may take such action by air, sea or land forces as may be necessary to maintain or restore international peace and security. Such action may include demonstrations, blockade, and other operations by air, sea and land forces of Members of the United Nations.

Article 43
1. All Members of the United Nations, in order to contribute to the maintenance of international peace and security, undertake to make available to the Security Council, on its call and in accordance with a special agreement or agreements, armed forces, assistance and facilities, including rights of passage, necessary for the purpose of maintaining international peace and security.
2. Such agreement or agreements shall govern the numbers and types of forces, their degree of readiness and general location, and the nature of the facilities and assistance to be provided.

3. The agreement or agreements shall be negotiated as soon as possible on the initiative of the Security Council. They shall be concluded between the Security Council and Members or between the Security Council and groups of Members and shall be subject to ratification by the signatory states in accordance with their respective constitutional processes.

Article 44

When the Security Council has decided to use force it shall, before calling on a Member not represented on it to provide armed forces in fulfilment of the obligations assumed under Article 43, invite that Member, if the Member so desires, to participate in the decisions of the Security Council concerning the employment of contingents of that Member's armed forces.

Article 45

In order to enable the United Nations to take urgent military measures, Members shall hold immediately available national air-force contingents for combined international enforcement action. The strength and degree of readiness of these contingents and plans for their combined action shall be determined ... by the Security Council with the assistance of the Military Staff Committee. [...]

Article 47

1. There shall be established a Military Staff Committee to advise and assist the Security Council on all questions relating to the Security Council's military requirements for the maintenance of international peace and security, the employment and command of forces placed at its disposal, the regulation of armaments, and possible disarmament.

2. The Military Staff Committee shall consist of the Chiefs of Staff of the permanent members of the Security Council or their representatives ...

3. The Military Staff Committee shall be responsible under the Security Council for the strategic direction of any armed forces placed at the disposal of the Security Council. Questions relating to the command of such forces shall be worked out subsequently.

4. The Military Staff Committee, with the authorization of the Security Council and after consultation with appropriate regional agencies, may establish regional sub-committees.

Article 48

1. The action required to carry out the decisions of the Security Council for the maintenance of international peace and security shall be taken by all Members of the United Nations or by some of them as the Security Council may determine ...

Article 49

The Members of the United Nations shall join in affording mutual assistance in carrying out the measures decided upon by the Security Council. [...]

Article 51

Nothing in the present Charter shall impair the inherent right of individual or collective self-defence if an armed attack occurs against a Member state of the United Nations, until the Security Council has taken measures necessary to maintain international peace and security. Measures taken by Members in the exercise of this right of self-defence shall be immediately reported to the Security Council and shall not in any way affect the authority and responsibility of the Security Council under the present Charter to take at any time such action as it deems necessary in order to maintain or restore international peace and security.

(ii)   *Collective security as originally conceived had a regional dimension. According to Chapter VIII, 'Regional Arrangements', local inter-governmental agencies might act as an enforcement arm of the Security Council. In the post-cold war years some joint operations have taken place but inter-agency relationships can be difficult – as was clear from the UN–NATO arrangement in Bosnia.*

Article 52

[...]
3.   The Security Council shall encourage the development of pacific settlement of local disputes through such regional arrangements or by such regional agencies either on the initiative of the states concerned or by reference from the Security Council. ...

Article 53

1.   The Security Council shall, where appropriate, utilize such regional arrangements or agencies for enforcement action under its authority. But no enforcement action shall be taken under regional arrangements or by regional agencies without the authorization of the Security Council ...

(iii)   *In contrast to collective security, the concept of peacekeeping is not specifically recognized in the Charter. It has been suggested that some legal base to peacekeeping might be found in Chapter VI, 'The Pacific Settlement of Disputes'.*

Article 33

1.   The parties to any dispute, the continuance of which is likely to endanger the maintenance of international peace and security, shall, first of all, seek a solution by negotiation, enquiry, mediation, conciliation, arbitration, judicial settlement, resort to regional agencies or arrangements, or other peaceful means of their choice.
2.   The Security Council shall, when it deems necessary, call upon the parties to settle their dispute by such means.

Article 34

The Security Council may investigate any dispute, or any situation which might lead to international friction or give rise to a dispute, in order to determine whether the continuance of the dispute or situation is likely to endanger the maintenance of international peace and security.

[...]

Article 36

1. The Security Council may, at any stage of a dispute ... recommend appropriate procedures or methods of adjustment. ...

Article 37

1. Should the parties to a dispute of the nature referred to in Article 33 fail to settle it by the means indicated in that Article, they shall refer it to the Security Council.

2. If the Security Council deems that the continuance of the dispute is in fact likely to endanger international peace and security, it shall decide whether to take action under Article 36 or to recommend such terms of settlement as it may consider appropriate.

(iv) *The crisis over the financing of peacekeeping operations which came to a head in the early 1960s turned on interpretations of Chapter IV of the Charter which dealt with the powers of the General Assembly. The Soviet Union (along with France) refused to accept that peacekeeping costs should be distributed according to Article 17 as security matters were the sole responsibility of the Security Council. In response the United States threatened to invoke Article 19 which deprived those in default of voting rights in the Assembly.*

Article 17

1 The General Assembly shall consider and approve the budget of the Organization.

2. The expenses of the Organization shall be borne by the Members as apportioned by the General Assembly.

Article 19

A Member of the United Nations which is in arrears in the payment of its financial contributions to the Organization shall have no vote in the General Assembly if the amount of its arrears equals or exceeds the amount of the contributions due to it for the preceding two full years. The General Assembly may, nevertheless, permit such a Member to vote if it is satisfied that the failure to pay is due to conditions beyond the control of the Member.

Charter of the United Nations.

DOCUMENT 4   THE SOVIET UNION AND THE VETO

Throughout the planning process for the United Nations the Soviet Union insisted that power should be concentrated in the Security Council. Here the Soviet representative at San Francisco (and future long-serving Soviet foreign minister), Andrei Gromyko, recalls his determination to resist any attempt by the west and the smaller powers to readjust the internal balance of power in the UN in favour of the General Assembly.

The USSR argued that all important issues of war and peace should go to the Security Council. Washington and London – supported by the representatives of many, mostly smaller, countries – argued for the division that would give the General Assembly more rights and the Security Council fewer. This attempt to hand over many of the Security Council's powers to the General Assembly was based on America's confidence that it could easily obtain a majority there and so put through any resolutions it liked. The clear result of this tendency would be to shift the balance of responsibility for the preservation of peace from the Security Council to the General Assembly, and the line separating each body hence became a major issue.

Tension grew steadily at the five power meetings as it became clear that President Truman had issued directives which cut straight across the Yalta agreements, and the US-British position on the division of powers was not going to be reconciled with the Soviet position unless one side gave way.

A host of resolutions now poured forth giving the General Assembly the right to review virtually any question that was not concerned with sanctions against a state. But Stettinius [the US secretary of state] was basically sympathetic to the Soviet Union's position that there should be a proper division of powers, and, after some tough talking, a possible agreement emerged: the Assembly would be able to discuss any question put by any state or group of states, but it could only issue a consultative opinion, and it would be for the Council to take binding decisions.

The Soviet delegation further declared: 'Our country will not agree to any UN Charter that might sow the seeds of a new military conflict.' The opponents of the [Security Council] veto then gave in. Everyone relaxed; jokes became more frequent. In just a few days the climate had changed. Clause 10 of chapter IV of the Charter appeared, limiting the powers of the General Assembly ...

Andrei Gromyko, *Memories* (London: Hutchinson, 1989), p. 120.

DOCUMENT 5   THE UNIFIED COMMAND IN KOREA

The 'UN' identity of the anti-North Korean alliance was distinctly ambiguous. In all essentials it was an American-led coalition, as is made clear in this memo of 13 September 1950 from the US state department to the American mission at the UN on the processing of offers of military assistance to South Korea. Effectively, the UN was merely a message carrier between the US and its allies.

1.   Offers of military assistance from member gvts will be transmitted to the SYG [secretary-general] of the UN who, in turn, will transmit the offers to the Unified Command (USG) [United States Government] through the US mission to the UN. Requests from the Unified Command (USG) for additional effective assistance in Korea may be transmitted to SYG for communication to the permanent delegations of the member govts.

2.   Upon receipt of the offer the Unified Command (USG) will enter into direct negotiations with the member govts concerned regarding details of the offer and its utilization or in respect to other effective assistance which the member govt might be in a position to provide.

3.   Upon completion of direct negotiations the Unified Command (USG) will inform the SYG of their results. This SYG will transmit this info to the delegation of the member govt concerned and, in consultation with the Unified Command (USG) and the delegation concerned, will release this info to the press.

US Department of State, *The Foreign Relations of the United States, 1950,* Vol. VII (Washington DC: US Government Printing Office, 1976), p. 776.

DOCUMENT 6   THE 'UNITING FOR PEACE' RESOLUTION

The return of the Soviet delegation to the Security Council in August 1950 ended the interlude in which the western powers could make decisions unhindered by the veto. In response the United States sought to open the way for issues blocked in the Security Council to be passed to the General Assembly for determination through a so-called 'Uniting for Peace' procedure. This amounted to an amendment to the Charter in an area of primary concern to the Soviet Union (see Document 4 above).

THE GENERAL ASSEMBLY
1.   *Resolves* that if the Security Council, because of lack of unanimity of the permanent members, fails to exercise its primary responsibility for the maintenance of international peace and security in any case where there appears to be a threat to the peace, breach of the peace, or act of aggression, the General Assembly shall consider the matter immediately with a view to making appro-

priate recommendations to Members for collective measures, including in the case of a breach of the peace or act of aggression the use of armed force when necessary, to maintain or restore international peace and security. If not in session at the time, the General Assembly may meet in emergency special session within twenty four hours of the request therefor. Such emergency special session shall be called if requested by the Security Council on the vote of any seven members, or by a majority of the members of the United Nations.

2. *Adopts* for this purpose ... amendments to its rules of procedure ...

UN Document GA/RES/377A [V], 3 November 1950.

DOCUMENT 7   **THE FORMATION OF UNTSO AND THE DEATH OF COUNT BERNADOTTE**

The United Nations Truce Supervision Organization in Palestine could in some respects be described as the first UN 'peacekeeping' operation. It was established in June 1948 on the initiative of the UN Mediator for Palestine, Count Folke Bernadotte, who shortly afterwards was murdered by Jewish extremists. Here the UN's first secretary-general, Trygve Lie, recalls this first peace mission and the death of its founder.

Count Bernadotte had requested me earlier to supply some military personnel to assist him in truce control functions, and I arranged with the three governments represented on the Security Council's Truce Commission – Belgium, France, and the United States – to assign officers from their armed forces for duty as United Nations military observers. During the second truce the number reached five hundred. They were stationed at strategic points along the cease-fire line and in the capitals of Israel and the Arab states. No story of United Nations effort in Palestine would be complete without a tribute to these gallant men who, without any previous experience in international teamwork, welded themselves in a matter of days into an effective team of United Nations officials. Their only protection was the modest blue-and-white armband added to their national uniform to identify them as United Nations observers. There was no risk they refused to take in the service of peace.

[...]

The shock was inexpressible. Ralph Bunche [a senior UN official in Palestine who was to succeed Bernadotte as Mediator] cabled that Count Bernadotte had been 'brutally assassinated by Jewish assailants of unknown identity in a planned, cold-blooded attack in the new city of Jerusalem at 14.05 GMT today, Friday 17 September'. The terrorism which had stained the Zionist cause had taken its noblest victim ... I knew the Count and his family personally, and this was enough to give a special edge to my sorrow. But my pain was refined by the reflection that the Count had died for the cause of the United Nations.

The bodies of Count Bernadotte and Colonel Serot [a French military observer who had died with him] were flown to Paris and that of the Count on to Stockholm. There was a memorial service at Orly airport for him and Colonel Serot, and for six other United Nations personnel who had been killed in Palestine either by the Arabs or by the Israelis. I flew to Stockholm for the funeral. The ceremonies were deeply moving. Count Bernadotte's uncle, the ninety-year-old King, was in attendance. Countess Bernadotte bore the tragedy of her husband's death with a dignity and nobility which seemed to symbolise the dedications to public service so characteristic not only of Count Bernadotte himself, but of his whole family.

Trygve Lie, *In the Cause of Peace: Seven Years with the United Nations* (New York: Macmillan, 1954), p. 187; pp. 190–1.

DOCUMENT 8   **LESTER PEARSON AND THE CREATION OF UNEF**

The foreign minister of Canada, Lester Pearson, played a key role leading up to the establishment of the United Nations Emergency Force for Suez in 1956. Here he describes the delicate behind-the-scenes diplomacy in New York which prefigured the General Assembly vote.

We had to sense the atmosphere in New York and, particularly, find out what the British were thinking. (The French were standing pat.) I had seen the British Acting High Commissioner [ambassador] in Ottawa the evening before I left for New York. Now I saw Sir Pierson Dixon, the British Ambassador to the United Nations, an old friend for whom I had great admiration, and told him we were contemplating some kind of initiative. I also talked by telephone with Norman Robertson [Canadian High Commissioner in London] who ... had told Kirkpatrick [Permanent Under-Secretary at the Foreign Office] that I was turning over in my mind the possibility of proposing a cease-fire ... He had also told him that, as part of this approach, it would be essential to set up an adequate UN military force to separate the Egyptians from the Israelis pending a stable and peaceful settlement of outstanding Middle Eastern questions.

We had learned in advance of Eden's [the British prime minister] intention to state in the British House of Commons that 'police action ... must be to separate the belligerents and to prevent the resumption of hostilities between them. If the UN were willing to take over the physical task of maintaining peace, no one would be better pleased than we.' It was not much but it was something. We took it to mean that Britain and France would be prepared to hand over the 'police task' they had assumed to a UN force. ... I knew that we would have to have something more to offer than just a diplomatic gimmick to meet Anglo-French requirements; another observer corps would not do. ...

By midnight [on 1 November] we had a fairly good idea that a UN peace-keeping intervention would be well-supported. If you like we had begun to mount a diplomatic operation on the assumption that we might decide to introduce a resolution for a cease-fire, to be policed by a United Nations emergency force ...

John A. Munro and Alex I. Inglis (eds), *Mike: The Memoirs of the Right Honourable Lester B. Pearson, Vol. 2 1948–1957* (Toronto: University of Toronto Press, 1973), pp. 245–6.

DOCUMENT 9   HAMMARSKJÖLD'S 'SUMMARY STUDY' –
                PEACEKEEPING CONCEPTUALIZED

In 1958, two years after the establishment of UNEF, the UN secretary-general Dag Hammarskjöld submitted a lengthy report to the General Assembly on the experience and lessons of the operation. This 'Summary Study' set out a series of principles relating to key aspects of the peacekeeping process such as host state consent, the appropriate type of contributing state, freedom of movement, political neutrality and financing. These, in Hammarskjöld's view, should form the basis of a peacekeeping 'model'.

B. *Basic Principles*
155.   As the arrangements discussed in this report do not cover the type of force envisaged under Chapter VII of the Charter, it follows from international law and the Charter that the United Nations cannot undertake to implement them by stationing units on the territory of a Member State without the consent of the Government concerned. It similarly follows from the Charter that the consent of a Member nation is necessary for the United Nations to use its military force or *materiel*. These basic rules have been observed in the recent United Nations operations in the Middle East. They naturally hold valid for all similar operations in the future. [...]
160.   Another point of principle which arises in relation to the question of consent refers to the composition of United Nations military elements stationed on the territory of a Member country. While the United Nations must reserve for itself the authority to decide on the composition of such elements, it is obvious that the host country, in giving its consent, cannot be indifferent to the composition of these elements. In order to limit the scope of possible difference of opinion, the United Nations in recent operations has followed two principles: not to include units from any of the permanent members of the Security Council; and not to include units from any country which, because of its geographical position or for other reasons, might be considered as possibly having a special interest in the situation which has called for the operation. I believe that these two principles should also be considered as essential to any stand-by arrangements.
[...]

164. Another principle in the UNEF status Agreement which should be retained is that the United Nations activity should have freedom of movement within its area of operations and all such facilities regarding access to that area and communications as are necessary for successful completion of the task. ...

165. ... [A]uthority granted to the United Nations group cannot be exercised within a given territory either in competition with representatives of the host Government or in co-operation with them on the basis of any joint operation. Thus a United Nations operation must be separate and distinct from activities by national authorities ...

166. A rule closely related to the one last mentioned, and reflecting a basic Charter principle, precludes the employment of United Nations elements in situations of an essentially internal nature. As a matter of course, the United Nations personnel cannot be permitted in any sense to be a party to internal conflicts. Their role must be limited to external aspects of the political situation as, for example, infiltration or other activities affecting international boundaries.

167. Even in the case of UNEF, where the United Nations itself had taken a stand on decisive elements in the situation which gave rise to the creation of the Force, it was explicitly stated that the Force should not be used to enforce any specific political solution of pending problems or to influence the political balance decisive to such a solution. This precept would clearly impose a serious limitation on the possible use of United Nations elements, were it to be given general application to them whenever they are not created under Chapter VII of the Charter. However, I believe its acceptance to be necessary, if the United Nations is to be in a position to draw on Member countries for contributions in men and *materiel* to United Nations operations of this kind. [...]

179. ... It should be generally recognized that [a right of self-defence for peacekeeping forces] exists. However, in certain cases this right should be exercised only under strictly defined conditions. A problem arises in this context because of the fact that a wide interpretation of the right of self-defence might well blur the distinction between operations of the character discussed in this report and combat operations, which would require a decision under Chapter VII of the Charter ... A reasonable definition seems to have been established in the case of UNEF, where the rule is applied that men engaged in the operation may never take the initiative in the use of armed force, but are entitled to respond with force to an attack with arms ... The basic element involved is clearly the prohibition against any *initiative* in the use of·armed force. This definition of the limit between self-defence, as permissible for United Nations elements of the kind discussed, and offensive action, which is beyond the competence of such elements, should be approved for future guidance. [...]

189. I believe that ... it should be established that the costs for United Nations operations of the type in question, based on decisions of the General Assembly or Security Council, should be allocated in accordance with the normal scale of contributions. The United Nations in this way should assume

responsibility for all additional costs incurred by a contributing country because of its participation in the operation, on the basis of a cost assessment which, on the other hand, would not transfer to the United Nations any costs which would otherwise have been incurred by a contributing Government under its regular national policy.

UN Document A/3943, 9 October 1958.

DOCUMENT 10   THREE SECURITY COUNCIL RESOLUTIONS ON THE CONGO

The rapidly shifting complexities of the Congo crisis and the UN's intervention in it are reflected in these successive Security Council mandates.

(i)   *When the operation was established in July 1960 the UN's role was seen simply as facilitating the withdrawal of Belgian forces and the provision of technical assistance.*

The Security Council
Considering the report of the Secretary-General on a request for a United Nations action in relation to the Republic of the Congo,
Considering the request for military assistance addressed to the Secretary-General by the President and Prime Minister of the Congo
1.   *Calls upon* the Government of Belgium to withdraw its troops from the territory of the Republic of the Congo;
2.   *Decides* to authorize the Secretary-General to take the necessary steps, in consultation with the Government of the Congo, to provide the Government with such military assistance as may be necessary until, through the efforts of the Congolese Government with the technical assistance of the United Nations, the national security forces may be able, in the opinion of the Government, to meet fully their tasks;
3.   *Requests* the Secretary-General to report to the Security Council as appropriate.

UN Document S/RES/143, 14 July 1960 (passed 8:0 with China, France and UK abstaining).

(ii)   *By the following February prime minister Lumumba had been murdered in Katanga, whose mercenary-backed secession from the Congo seemed, particularly to the Afro-Asian bloc, to be insufficiently opposed by the UN. A more robust response on the part of ONUC was now approved by the Security Council. The border between peacekeeping and enforcement was now becoming blurred.*

The Security Council

[...]

1.   *Urges* that the United Nations take immediately all appropriate measures to prevent the occurrence of civil war in the Congo, including arrangements for cease-fires, the halting of all military operations, the prevention of clashes and the use of force, if necessary, in the last resort;

2.   *Urges* that measures be taken for the immediate withdrawal and evacuation from the Congo of all Belgian and other foreign military and paramilitary personnel and political advisers not under the United Nations Command, and mercenaries;

3.   *Calls upon* all states to take immediate and energetic measures to prevent the departure of such personnel for the Congo from their territories, and for the denial of transit and other facilities to them;

4.   *Decides* that an immediate and impartial investigation be held in order to ascertain the circumstances of the death of Mr Lumumba and his colleagues and that the perpetrators of these crimes be punished ...

UN Document S/RES/161, 21 February 1961 (passed 9:0 with France and USSR abstaining).

(iii)   *In November 1961, following the death of Hammarskjöld, the Security Council responded to the continuing defiance of separatist Katanga with a still stronger 'enforcement-orientated' resolution.*

The Security Council

[...]

1.   *Strongly deprecates* the secessionist activities illegally carried out by the provincial administration of Katanga, with the aid of external resources and manned by foreign mercenaries;

2.   *Further deprecates* the armed action against United Nations forces and personnel in pursuit of such activities;

3.   *Insists* that such activities shall cease forthwith, *and calls* upon all concerned to desist therefrom;

4.   *Authorizes* the Secretary-General to take vigorous action, including the use of the requisite measure of force, if necessary, for the immediate apprehension, detention pending legal action and/or deportation of all foreign military and paramilitary personnel and political advisers not under the United Nations Command, and mercenaries;

[...]

8.   *Declares* that all secessionist activities against the Republic of the Congo are contrary to ... Security Council decisions and specifically *demands* that such activities that are now taking place in Katanga shall cease forthwith ...

UN Document S/RES/169, 24 November 1961 (passed 9:0 with France and UK abstaining).

DOCUMENT 11   KHRUSHCHEV CALLS FOR THE ABOLITION
OF THE OFFICE OF SECRETARY-GENERAL

Within a few months of its creation the United Nations operation in the Congo seemed to have aggravated rather than eased east–west relations. Moscow claimed that the UN under secretary-general Hammarskjöld had become an instrument of western 'imperialism' in the Congo. The Soviet leader, Nikita Khrushchev, called for a fundamental reform of the organization's management. In a speech to the General Assembly in September 1960 he proposed the replacement of the office of secretary-general with a 'troika' composed of representatives of the west, the eastern bloc and the Afro-Asian group.

(...)

280.   The Soviet Union considers that if a correct approach is taken to the utilization of ... international armed forces, they may indeed be useful. But the experience of the Congo puts us on our guard. That experience indicates that the United Nations forces are being utilized exactly in the way against which we warned, a way we emphatically oppose. Mr Hammarskjöld ... has taken a position of purely formal condemnation of the colonialists. In actual practice, however, he is following the colonialists' line, opposing the lawful government of the Congo and the Congolese people and supporting the renegades who, under the guise of fighting for the independence of the republic of the Congo, are actually continuing the policy of the colonialists and are evidently receiving some reward from them for their treachery.

281.   What is to be done in this case? If this is how the international armed forces are to be used in practice, to suppress liberation movements, it will naturally be difficult to reach agreement on their establishment, since there will be no guarantee that they will not be used for reactionary purposes that are alien to the interests of peace. Provision must be made to ensure that no state falls into the predicament in which the Republic of the Congo now finds itself. We are convinced that other States also realize this danger. Solutions must therefore be sought which would preclude similar occurrences in the future.

282.   The Soviet Government has come to a definite conclusion on this matter and wishes to expound its point of view before the United Nations General Assembly. Conditions have clearly matured to the point where the post of Secretary-General, who alone directs the staff and alone interprets and executes the decisions of the Security Council and the sessions of the General Assembly, should be abolished. It would be expedient to abandon the system under which all practical work in the intervals between General Assembly sessions and Security Council meetings is determined by the Secretary-General alone.

283.   The executive organ of the United Nations should reflect the real situation that obtains in the world today. The United Nations includes States

which are members of the military blocs of the Western Powers, socialist States and neutralist [Non-Aligned] countries. It would therefore be completely justified to take that situation into account, and we would be better safeguarded against the negative developments which have come to light in the work of the United Nations, especially during the recent events in the Congo.

284. We consider it reasonable and just for the executive organ of the United Nations to consist not of a single person – the Secretary-General – but of three persons invested with the highest trust of the United Nations, persons representing the States belonging to the military block of the Western Powers, the socialist States and the neutralist States. This composition of the United Nations executive organ would create conditions for a more correct implementation of the decisions taken.

285. In brief, we consider it advisable to set up, in the place of a Secretary-General who is at present the interpreter and executor of the decisions of the General Assembly and the Security Council, a collective executive organ of the United Nations consisting of three persons each of whom would represent a certain group of States. That would provide a definite guarantee that the work of the United Nations executive organ would not be carried on to the detriment of any one of these groups of States. The United Nations executive organ would then be a genuinely democratic organ; it would really guard the interests of all States Members of the United Nations irrespective of the social and political system of any particular Member State. This is particularly necessary at the present time, and it would be even more so in the future.

[...]

UN Document A/PV.869, 23 September 1960.

DOCUMENT 12   'KHRUSHCHEV REMEMBERS' THE FAILURE
OF THE TROIKA PROPOSAL

The Soviet Union's radical proposals for the restructuring of the UN secretariat found little favour with the Afro-Asian members of the General Assembly. The support of this growing and increasingly influential Non-Aligned bloc was essential if the troika idea was to be adopted. Consequently, Khrushchev retreated. Recalling the issue several years later, after he had been ousted from the Kremlin, he still maintained that the troika idea had been a sound one.

Some people who thought they were pretty smart kept trying to convince me that my idea wasn't possible, and even some who were friendly towards us insisted that having three heads of the UN would paralyse the organization. But I was convinced I was right and promoted the idea enthusiastically. After all, why should three leaders 'paralyze' the UN? Look at the Security Council: it has fifteen members, including five permanent ones with veto power. Why shouldn't the Secretariat be administered in the same way, headed by a troika which would take into account the interests of all three sides, rather than just one side? No doubt, it would sometimes take a bit longer to act on certain matters, but perhaps in some cases that would be just as well. Sometimes it would be better not to have a question solved at all than to have it solved by one man who is under the influence of the capitalist countries. To look at it realistically, we had no hope of having a Secretary-General who was a Communist – or even a non-Communist promoted by our socialist camp. The capitalist countries would never have stood for it. So why shouldn't we have at least one representative among three to guard our interests in the Secretariat?

Unfortunately, we were never able to get very far with this proposal because the capitalist countries were against us and made the nonaligned countries come over to their side. So the idea failed to win support on the testing ground of the General Assembly. We had a real fight with Hammarskjöld, and our relations with him went down the drain.

N.S. Khrushchev, *Khrushchev Remembers: The Last Testament*, trans. and ed. Strobe Talbot (London: André Deutsch, 1974), pp. 483–4.

DOCUMENT 13   THE CONGO: CONOR CRUISE O'BRIEN
AND THE ROLE OF THE UN

The military operations ordered by Conor Cruise O'Brien, the UN represent- ative in Katanga, against the western-backed secessionists in August and Sep- tember 1961 led indirectly to Hammarskjöld's death when he travelled to the Congo to deal with the ensuing crisis. Following his dismissal from UN serv- ice after these events O'Brien wrote an elegant apologia *for his actions. In this he portrayed Hammarskjöld himself as favouring firm action against Katanga, in order to refute accusations that he (O'Brien) had acted without authorization. Here he recalls his initiation by Rajeshwar Dayal into the fraught international politics surrounding the Katanga affair.*

By any reckoning there were storms ahead. The captain's problem in setting his course was to decide which storm-centre presented on the whole the lesser risk. In deciding as he did on the 'Afro-Asian interpretation' – the vigorous implementation of the February resolution [authorizing the use of force by ONUC 'to prevent the occurrence of civil war'] – Mr Hammarskjöld decided to head for the storm centring on the English Channel – that is to say, to risk the hostility of England, France and Belgium. He may have underestimated the dangers of this course; he was surely right in considering it less dangerous – to the United Nations, to the Congo and to general peace – than the alterna- tive of drifting towards collapse.

At the time I was aware of these storm signals, but that does not mean that I had much idea of what the fury of the storm, when actually experienced, would be like. ... There were some whitened bones around ... which should have brought things home to me.

Mr Dayal was just leaving ... to rejoin the Indian Foreign Service. He was leaving at his own request, following his 'controversial' term of office as UN Special Representative in the Congo ... He explained without rancour, but as things important for me to know, the basic reasons for his departure. Every great power, he explained, wished to turn the United Nations into an instrument of its own policy, but some powers were in a better position than others to do so. In his time in Leopoldville ... the powers in the best position to make this use of the United Nations were the United States and, secondarily, Britain. Ambassadors of these powers, effectively – though not always in unison – controlled President Kasavubu and General Mobutu, and they were therefore most anxious that the United Nations should accept these gentlemen's nominees as being the Government of the Congo. As the legality of all this was highly questionable, and as it represented the viewpoint of only one group of powers within the United Nations, Mr Dayal had held out against it and in favour of the convening of parliament and the election of a government of unquestioned legality. In this stand he was supported by the Secretary-General.

Conor Cruise O'Brien, *To Katanga and Back: A UN Case History* (London: Hutchinson, 1962), pp. 63–4.

DOCUMENT 14   HAMMARSKJÖLD AND THE CONGO: THE
PRESSURES OF OFFICE

Assailed from all sides over the Congo, the stress on the solitary and cerebral Hammarskjöld over the year leading up to his death in September 1961 was immense. Some indication of his state of mind can be detected in the verse he wrote at the time and which was published after he died.

July 6th, 61
Tired
And lonely,
So tired
The heart aches.
Meltwater trickles
Down the rocks,
The fingers are numb,
The knees tremble.
It is now,
Now, that you must not give in.

On the path of the others
Are resting places,
Places in the sun
Where they can meet.
But this
Is your path,
And it is now,
Now, that you must not fail.

Weep
If you can,
Weep,
But do not complain.
The way chose you –
And you must be thankful.

Dag Hammarskjöld, *Markings*, [trans. Leif Sjöberg and W.H. Auden], (London: Faber & Faber, 1964), p. 175.

DOCUMENT 15   FORMING THE CYPRUS FORCE

In March 1964 secretary-general U Thant encountered initial wariness on the part of potential contributors to UNFICYP. Behind this lay the experience of the Congo and a perception that the Cyprus crisis might be even more militarily and politically fraught. There was also concern at the uncertainty over financing. These worries are evident in the reply from the Irish Minister for External Affairs, Frank Aiken, to U Thant's initial request for troops. In addition to misgivings held in common with all potential contributors, Ireland had a special 'national' concern over the prospect of the partition of Cyprus.

13 March 1964

Excellency,

I have received your telegram this morning about your efforts to implement the resolution of the Security Council of 4 March 1964, dealing with the establishment of a United Nations peace-keeping force in Cyprus. I have also received the text of replies you have given to the requests for clarification made to you by some of the countries asked to participate in the force.

As your telegram so generously recognises, Ireland as a faithful member of the United Nations has invariably given its whole-hearted support to the peace-keeping efforts of the United Nations. It was in this spirit that my Government examined sympathetically your request for an Irish contingent for the United Nations peace-keeping force in Cyprus. I am authorised to give you the following reply to your request.

The Government of Ireland have agreed in principle, subject to the adoption by Dáil Eireann [the Irish parliament] of the resolution required by Irish law, to comply with the Secretary-General's request to contribute a battalion of approximately 500 men to the United Nations peace-keeping force in Cyprus.

This decision is conditional on the Government's understanding:

1) that the function of the force will be to maintain peace while the process to achieve an agreed solution of the problem confronting Cyprus is in progress and that the force will have no function in influencing the character of the settlement to be made or its subsequent enforcement;

2) that an assurance will be forthcoming from the Governments of Great Britain, Greece and Turkey that, during the presence of the force in Cyprus, they will not intervene or attempt to impose by force, or by threat of force, a solution of the problem – and, particularly, a solution by partition;

3) that every effort will be made by the Secretary-General to ensure that the Greek and Turkish Governments will place under the command of the United Nations their troops now stationed in Cyprus; and

4) that if it should be agreed to be necessary to keep a United Nations force in Cyprus after the expiration of three months,

    a) other member countries of the United Nations would be asked to provide contingents and

    b) the Government would be free to withdraw the Irish contingent, irrespective of the progress of the mediation and the state of affairs in Cyprus at that time.

The Irish Government view with regret the decision to raise funds on a voluntary basis for a United Nations peace-keeping force. They regard it as a grave and unwise departure from the principle of collective responsibility. Subject to Dáil approval the Government would pay the usual United Nations overseas allowances to our troops and would accept no reimbursement from the United Nations unless it were levied on all members of the United Nations in the normal way.

Subject to the foregoing and as soon as you inform me that you have received the assurance referred to in paragraph 4 above, my government will take the earliest opportunity of seeking the approval of the Dáil for sending a battalion to join the United Nations peace-keeping force in Cyprus.

Accept, Excellency, the renewed assurance of my highest consideration.

Frank Aiken

Minister for External Affairs

Bulletin of the Department of External Affairs of Ireland, No. 653, 23 March 1964.

DOCUMENT 16   THE INTERNATIONAL COURT OF JUSTICE
ON THE FINANCING OF PEACEKEEPING

The deepening crisis over the basis on which UN members paid for peace-keeping operations led to the issue being laid before the International Court of Justice for an advisory opinion in 1962 on the applicability of Article 17(ii) of the Charter (see Doc. 3(iv)). The Court, after detailed consideration of the legal bases of UNEF and ONUC, upheld by a majority decision the western position that peacekeeping was a 'normal' cost of the UN.

It is not possible to find in [the] description of the functions of UNEF, as outlined by the Secretary-General and concurred in by the General Assembly without a dissenting vote, any evidence that the [Suez] force was to be used for purposes of enforcement. Nor can such evidence be found in the subsequent operations of the force, operations which did not exceed the functions ascribed to it.

It could not therefore have been patent on the face of the [General Assembly enabling] resolution that the establishment of UNEF was in effect 'enforcement action' under Chapter VII which, in accordance with the Charter, could be authorized only by the Security Council.

On the other hand, it is apparent that the operations were undertaken to fulfil a prime purpose of the United Nations ... This being true, the Secretary-General properly exercised the authority given to him to incur financial obligations of the Organization and expenses resulting from such obligations must be considered 'expenses of the Organization within the meaning of Article 17. paragraph 2'.

[...]

The operations in the Congo were initially authorized by the Security Council in the resolution of 14 July 1960 [see *Doc. 10(i)*] which was adopted without a dissenting vote.

[...]

In the light of [this] ... it is impossible to reach the conclusion that the operations in question usurped or impinged upon the prerogatives conferred by the Charter on the Security Council. ...

It is not necessary for the Court to express an opinion as to which article or articles of the Charter were the basis for the resolutions of the Security Council but it can be said that the operations of ONUC did not include a use of armed force against a State which the Security Council, under Article 39, determined to have committed an act of aggression or to have breached the peace. The armed forces which were utilized in the Congo were not authorized to take military action against any State under Chapter VII and therefore did not constitute 'action' as that term is used in Article 11.

For the reasons stated, financial obligations which, in accordance with the clear and reiterated authority of both the Security Council and the General Assembly, the Secretary-General incurred on behalf of the United Nations,

constitute obligations of the Organization for which the General Assembly
was entitled to make provision under Article 17...

For these reasons,

THE COURT IS OF THE OPINION

by nine votes to five,

that the expenditures authorized ... constitute 'expenses of the Organization'
within the meaning of Article 17, paragraph 2, of the Charter of the United
Nations.

'Certain Expenses of the United Nations (Article 17, paragraph 2 of the Charter), Advisory Opinion of 20 July 1962', *ICJ Reports 1962.*

DOCUMENT 17   PEACEKEEPING FINANCE, THE 'ARTICLE 19
CRISIS'

*The Soviet Union and its allies refused to accept the judgement of the ICJ
(Document 16) and continued to withhold assessed financial contributions to
peacekeeping. In 1964 the United States threatened to invoke Article 19 of
the Charter which would have deprived those states in default of payments of
their General Assembly vote (see Doc. 3(iv)). The ensuing crisis is recalled
here by the secretary-general of the time, U Thant.*

The atmosphere at the United Nations in September and October 1964 was
one of utter gloom. There was the general feeling that the Organization
would find itself unable to meet on-going (including payroll) commitments.
Several representatives were even predicting that the United Nations would
have to shut down. To avert the crisis, the member states agreed to postpone
the opening of the Assembly to November 10 and then to December. I was
convinced, however, by the experience of the past three years, that a policy of
drift, of improvisation, of ad hoc solutions, and of reliance on the generosity
of the few rather than the collective responsibility of all, could not endure
much longer. ...

It was only at the last moment that we found a way to avert an immediate
confrontation. On the eve of the opening of the nineteenth session, agreement
was reached among the US, the USSR, France, and Britain on a formula
which would permit the Assembly to transact essential and noncontroversial
business by unanimous consent – that is, without taking a formal vote. When
the Assembly opened there was an understanding that issues other than those
that could be disposed of without objection would not be raised in the general
debates. The session proceeded without incident.

When the Assembly reconvened on January 18, 1965, the confrontation
was again averted when Adlai Stevenson, the US representative, declared that
in order to prevent the will of the majority from being 'frustrated by one
member', the United States would not invoke Article 19. The threat of a con-

frontation was finally lifted altogether in August 1965, when Stevenson's successor, Arthur J. Goldberg, told the Special Committee on Peacekeeping that the United States had decided reluctantly to bow to the will of the majority and refrain from invoking Article 19.

U Thant, *View from the UN* (New York: Doubleday, 1978), p. 90.

DOCUMENT 18   **DÉTENTE AND THE 1973 MIDDLE EAST WAR: THE US POSITION**

In the 1970s détente brought a new appreciation of mutual self-interest between the superpowers and they achieved a considerable degree of co-operation over the Middle East war in 1973. Here the US secretary of state at the time, Henry Kissinger, describes the initial co-ordination of policy with the Soviet Union which would eventually lead to the creation of UNEF II. It is clear in the extract, though, that national advantage was never far from the calculations of the superpowers.

A message was received from Brezhnev [the Soviet leader] early Monday, October 8: 'We have contacted the leaders of the Arab states on the question of cease-fire. We hope to get a reply shortly. We feel that we should act in cooperation with you, being guided by the broad interests of maintaining peace and developing the Soviet-American relations [*sic*]. We hope that President Nixon will act likewise'.

When Dobrynin [the Soviet ambassador in Washington – see *Doc. 19*] read me Brezhnev's message on the phone, I thought it served our immediate purpose very well. Since we did not intend to introduce a resolution and the Soviet Union was offering to coordinate with us, we were certain to get through the day without confrontation or embarrassing proposals. By the next day, we were convinced, the Israeli offensive would prevail; the Security Council would then call for a cease-fire in place. Our ally would have repulsed an attack by Soviet weapons. We could begin our peace process with the Arabs on the proposition that we had stopped an Israeli advance and with the Israelis on the basis that we had been steadfastly at their side in the crisis. I therefore did not hesitate to tell Dobrynin that we would act in the spirit of Brezhnev's message. We would put forward no resolution that day, nor without giving the Soviet Union several hours' advance warning. We would instruct Ambassador Scali [the US representative] to speak philosophically in the Security Council; we would avoid inflammatory statements. We expected the Soviet Union to follow a similar course. Dobrynin agreed.

Henry Kissinger, *Years of Upheaval* (London: Weidenfeld and Nicolson, 1982), pp. 486–7.

DOCUMENT 19   DÉTENTE AND THE 1973 MIDDLE EAST
WAR: THE SOVIET POSITION

The Soviet Union's reaction to the 1973 Middle East war and the implications for superpower détente are here recalled by Anatoly Dobrynin, Moscow's veteran ambassador to Washington.

Kissinger was already in New York for the annual session of the United Nations General Assembly [when the war began], and he wanted to convoke the Security Council. He wanted both the Soviet and the American representatives to be instructed to take a measured position without siding entirely with their traditional clients. The United States, he said, intended to propose a resolution calling for a cease fire ...

Moscow replied promptly: 'The Soviet Union received reports about the beginning of hostilities in the Middle east [*sic*] simultaneously with you. ... We are considering, like you, possible steps to be taken to remedy the situation. We hope to communicate with you soon to coordinate our actions.'

Anatoly Dobrynin, *In Confidence: Moscow's Ambassador to America's Six Cold War Presidents* (New York: Times Books, 1995), p. 290.

DOCUMENT 20   KURT WALDHEIM ON THE LEBANON
FORCE

Here Kurt Waldheim, secretary-general in 1978, recalls the process of formation of UNIFIL and some of the political problems around its composition.

Speed was of the essence. The nearest available troops were the Austrian and Iranian contingents serving in UNDOF, the disengagement force on the Golan Heights. They could be transported overland by truck convoy and reach their new deployment area within a few hours. However, I could not transfer them without the consent of their governments.

I first contacted the Austrian government, which let me know that they rather preferred to have their troops stay where they were. So I turned to the Iranians. The Shah was still in power and had been most helpful in previous peace-keeping activities. I reached him easily on the telephone, he gave his assent, and within twenty-four hours the Iranian contingent was on its way. We withdrew the Swedes from UNEF and soon reached the approved strength of 4,000 men. General Erskine of Ghana was in command and strongly recommended an increase to 6,000. It was a prudent request. The force was operating in two largely separate and extensive areas, in rugged terrain and often in situations of great danger. Over the months, the Security Council agreed to a further reinforcement of up to 7,000 men.
[...]

The Netherlands government, traditionally friendly to the Israelis, provided a contingent, yet, when they began to take casualties in skirmishes with Major Haddad's Christian militia and the PLO, the Dutch began to criticise the Israelis for failing to control their satellite. The Netherlands government found it necessary to pacify growing domestic opposition over the casualties and over embroilment with the Israelis. Their contingent was finally withdrawn.

The French played an important part in UNIFIL from the first. They furnished more men for the force than any other single nation. An elite group of French paratroopers arrived among the very first contingents under the command of Colonel Salvan, a wounded veteran of the climactic Vietnam battle of Dien Bien Phu. He was appointed chief of staff to General Erskine, but a few months later his car was ambushed and he was seriously injured.

Kurt Waldheim, *In the Eye of the Storm* (London: Weidenfeld and Nicolson, 1985), pp. 189–90.

DOCUMENT 21   OPERATION DESERT STORM

Military action against Iraq to force its withdrawal from Kuwait was approved by the Security Council in November 1990. Although referring to Chapter VII, the Council did not invoke its legally binding collective security powers under Article 43 of the Charter. Operation Desert Storm was essentially an 'independent' alliance acting with UN authorization rather than a 'UN force'.

The Security Council
Acting under Chapter VII of the Charter;
1. *Demands* that Iraq comply fully [with previous resolutions calling for its withdrawal from Kuwait] and decides, while maintaining all its decisions, to allow Iraq one final opportunity as a pause of goodwill to do so;
2. *Authorizes* Member States co-operating with the Government of Kuwait, unless Iraq on or before January 15, 1991 fully implements the foregoing resolutions, to use all necessary means to uphold and implement Security Council Resolution 660 and all subsequent relevant resolutions and to restore international peace and security in the area;
3. *Requests* all States to provide appropriate support for the actions undertaken in pursuance of paragraph 2 of this resolution;
4. *Requests* the states concerned to keep the Council regularly informed of the progress of actions undertaken pursuant to paragraphs 2 and 3 of this resolution;
5. *Decides* to remain seized of the matter.

UN Document S/RES/678, 29 November 1990 (passed 12:2 with Cuba and Yemen voting against and China abstaining).

DOCUMENT 22   *AN AGENDA FOR PEACE*

In his major 1992 analysis of the current state and future prospects for peace-keeping, secretary-general Boutros Boutros-Ghali proposed the creation of a new type of UN force with a role between interposition and enforcement. It is helpful here to refer back to Document 3(i).

PEACE–ENFORCEMENT UNITS

44.   The mission of forces under Article 43 would be to respond to outright aggression, imminent or actual. Such forces are not likely to be available for some time to come. Cease-fires have often been agreed to but not complied with, and the United Nations has sometimes been called upon to send forces to restore and maintain the cease-fire. This task can on occasion exceed the mission of peace-keeping forces and the expectations of peace-keeping force contributors. I recommend that the Council consider the utilization of peace-enforcement units in clearly defined circumstances and with their terms of reference specified in advance. Such units from Member States would be available on call and would consist of troops that have volunteered for such service. They would have to be more heavily armed than peace-keeping forces and would have to undergo extensive preparatory training within their national forces. Deployment and operation of such forces would be under the authorization of the Security Council and would, as in the case of peace-keeping forces, be under the command of the Secretary-General. I consider such peace-enforcement units to be warranted as a provisional measure under Article 40 of the Charter. Such peace-enforcement units should not be confused with the forces that may eventually be constituted under Article 43 to deal with acts of aggression or with the military personnel which Governments may agree to keep on stand-by for possible contribution to peace-keeping operations.

Boutros Boutros-Ghali, *An Agenda for Peace: Preventive Diplomacy, Peace-making and Peace-keeping* (New York: United Nations, 1992), p. 26.

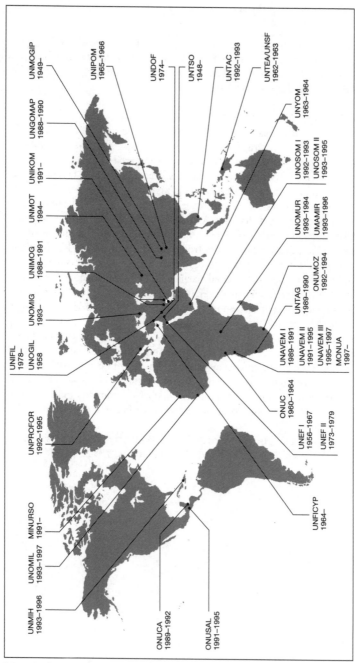

Map 1. UN Operations 1948–1998

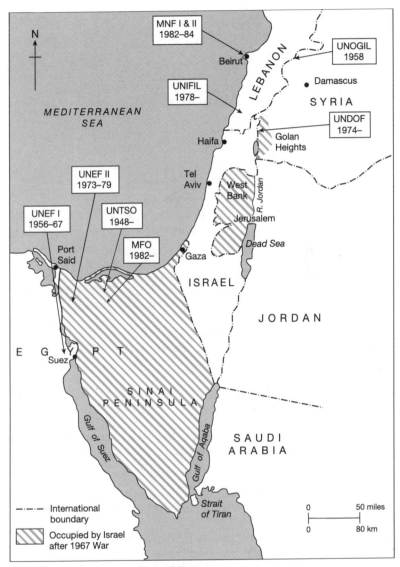

Map 2. Peacekeeping in the Middle East

GUIDE TO CHARACTERS

Aiken, Frank (1898–1983): Irish foreign minister 1957–69; a 'middle-power' activist at the UN and supporter of Irish army participation in peacekeeping operations.

Akashi, Yasushi (1931–): Japanese diplomat who was the UN representative in Bosnia during the civil war there. Widely criticized for his reluctance to authorize robust UN action against the Bosnian Serbs.

Andropov, Yuri (1914–84): Soviet leader 1982–1984; regarded as a reformer, though his early death in office prevented development of distinct policies.

Annan, Kofi (1938–): Ghanaian secretary-general of the UN; took office in 1997 succeeding Boutros-Ghali.

Assad, Hafiz (1930–): President of Syria from November 1970 (previously defence minister); negotiated deployment of UNDOF in 1974 with Henry Kissinger.

Aydeed, Mohammed Farah: Somali 'warlord'; leader of one of the largest armed factions confronting UNOSOM/UNITAF in 1992–95.

Barre, Siyad (1919–): Somali president between 1969 and 1991; supported by the US during the cold war; overthrown by opposition factions who then began to fight among themselves for control of the country.

Begin, Menachim (1913–92): Israeli prime minister 1977–83; leader of right-wing Likud Party; negotiated 1978 Camp David peace agreement with Egypt under American auspices.

Ben-Gurion, David (1886–1973): First prime minister of Israel 1948–63 and leader of Labour Party; in office during wars of 1948 and 1956.

Bernadotte, Count Folke (1895–1948): Swedish UN mediator in Palestine in 1948; had previously acted in various mediatory roles during the Second World War; assassinated by Jewish extremists in September 1948.

Boutros-Ghali, Boutros (1922–): Egyptian secretary-general of the UN 1992–97; in office during the post-cold war expansion of peacekeeping undertakings; published *An Agenda for Peace* in 1992.

Brezhnev, Leonid (1906–82): Soviet leader 1964–82; succeeded the deposed Khrushchev; ordered Soviet invasion of Czechoslovakia in 1968, though he also pursued a policy of détente with the west.

Bunche, Ralph (1904–71): Long-serving African-American UN official; involved in a range of peacemaking efforts from Palestine (where he succeeded Count Bernadotte as Mediator) to the Congo.

Burns, General E.L.M. (1897–1985): Canadian commander of UNEF from its formation in 1956 until 1959.

Bush, George (1924–): US president (Republican) 1988–92; in office during the Gulf War against Iraq and through the end of the cold war.

Cadogan, Sir Alexander (1884–1968): British diplomat and representative at Dumbarton Oaks conference in 1944; later British permanent representative at the UN.

Carter, Jimmy (1924–): US president (Democrat) 1976–80; a foreign policy liberal by American standards, he was the driving force behind 1978 Camp David agreement between Israel and Egypt.

Chamoun, Camille: Maronite Christian president of Lebanon during crisis of 1958 which led to creation of UNOGIL.

Chernenko, Konstantin (1911–85): Soviet leader in 1984–85 in interval between Andropov and Gorbachev.

Churchill, Winston S. (1874–1965): British leader during Second World War; prime minister in wartime coalition 1940–45 and then Conservative prime minister from 1951–55; signatory of Atlantic Charter in 1941 and closely involved in the creation of the UN.

Clinton, Bill (1946–): US president (Democrat) from 1992; inherited American involvement in Somalia from his predecessor (George Bush); urged international intervention in Haiti in early 1990s and robust action in Bosnia.

Cordier, Andrew: UN representative in the Congo capital Leopoldville in 1960; US citizen; accused of pro-western, anti-Lumumba actions during crisis of September of that year.

Dayal, Rajeshwar: Indian UN representative in the Congo 1960–61 in succession to Andrew Cordier; displayed a greater sensitivity to Afro-Asian concerns over the Congo than his predecessor.

De Gaulle, Charles (1890–1970):   Leader of the 'Free French' forces during Second World War and head of government 1944–46; president of France 1958–69; advocate of continued national sovereignty against any shift in international authority to an 'independent' UN.

Dobrynin, Anatoly (1919–):   Veteran Soviet ambassador in Washington; in office through a succession of cold war crises; helped co-ordinate Soviet response to 1973 Middle East war with that of the US and co-operated in arranging a UN peacekeeping response.

Dulles, John Foster (1888–1959):   Secretary of state during the (Republican) Eisenhower administration in the US during the 1950s; architect of the policy of 'containment' towards the Soviet Union.

Eden, Anthony (Earl of Avon) (1897–1977):   British Conservative foreign secretary before and during Second World War; prime minister 1955–57 when he conspired with Israel and France to attack Egypt after Nasser's nationalization of the Suez Canal in 1956; accepted the interposition of UNEF as a face-saving device to cover British withdrawal.

Eisenhower, Dwight D. (1890–1969):   US president (Republican) 1953–61; in office during the most glacial period of the cold war; critical of Britain and France over their actions in the Suez crisis of 1956.

Ford, Gerald (1913–):   US president (Republican) 1974–76; vice-president in Nixon administration; came to office after the fall of Nixon in the wake of the Watergate scandal.

Gorbachev, Mikhail (1931–):   Soviet president 1985–91; reformer who presided over the end of the cold war and the break-up of the Soviet Union.

Gromyko, Andrei (1909–):   Veteran Soviet diplomat and foreign minister; Soviet representative at Dumbarton Oaks conference in 1944; deputy foreign minister and UN representative 1946–52; Soviet foreign minister 1957–85.

Hammarskjöld, Dag (1905–61):   Swedish second secretary-general of the UN from 1953 until his death in Africa during the Congo crisis in 1961;

widely regarded as the 'founding father' of UN peacekeeping following the establishment of UNEF in 1956.

Johnson, Lyndon B. (1908–73):   US president (Democrat) 1963–69; elevated from the vice-presidency after the assassination of Kennedy and then elected in his own right; presided over deepening American involvement in Vietnam.

Kasavubu, Joseph (1910–69):   First president of the Congo 1960–65; pro-western rival of prime minister Patrice Lumumba but ultimately dependant on army chief Joseph Mobutu who eventually ousted him from the presidency and took his place.

Kennedy, John F. (1917–63):   US president (Democrat) from 1961 until his assassination in 1963; brought US policy on the Congo closer into line with the concerns of the Afro-Asian states in the UN; confronted the Soviet Union in the Cuban missile crisis of 1962.

Khrushchev, Nikita (1894–1971):   Prominent in collective Soviet leadership after the death of Stalin in 1953 and then leader in his own right from 1956 until being deposed in 1964. Suspicious of western dominance in the UN and particularly hostile to Hammarskjöld during the Congo crisis; advocated a bloc-based *troika* to replace the office of secretary-general.

Kim Il Sung (1912–94):   Communist leader of North Korea from 1948 until his death; invaded the south in 1950 precipitating the Korean War; object of huge personality cult who maintained North Korea in international isolation throughout his decades in power.

Kissinger, Henry (1923–):   American academic and politician; foreign policy adviser and then secretary of state during the Nixon and Ford administrations; oversaw the development of détente between the superpowers and 'co-opted' UN peacekeeping in its service, particularly in the Middle East in the 1970s.

Lie, Trygve (1896–1968):   Norwegian first secretary-general of the UN 1946–53. In office during the Korean War when his approach deepened Soviet suspicions of the UN's pro-western character.

Lumumba, Patrice (1925–61):   First prime minister of the Congo after its independence from Belgium; requested UN intervention in 1960, though soon became disaffected at the UN's supposed western bias and became increasingly pro-Soviet in his pronouncements; deposed in September 1960 and then captured and murdered by his political enemies.

MacArthur, General Douglas (1880–1964):   American commander in Asia during the Second World War; appointed to lead the 'UN' Unified Command in Korea in 1950; his increasingly 'independent' and 'political' behaviour caused concern both among the allies fighting in Korea and in Washington; dismissed by President Truman in 1951.

Makarios, Archbishop (1913–77):   Greek Cypriot first president of independent Cyprus from 1960; his attempts to enhance the constitutional and political power of his own ethnic community in 1963–64 led to the creation of UNFICYP; attempted coup against him by pro-Greek rightists in 1974 led to Turkish invasion and *de facto* partition.

Meir, Golda (1898–1978):   Israeli (Labour) prime minister 1969–74. In office during the war of 1973 and involved in the early stages of the subsequent US-brokered peace negotiations.

Mobutu, Joseph (Sese Seko) (1930–97):   Commander of Congolese army after independence from Belgium; instrumental in ousting and subsequent murder of Lumumba; presided over deeply corrupt, pro-western Congo (Zaire) from 1965 until 1997 when he was overthrown.

Molotov, Vyacheslav (1890–1986):   Soviet foreign minister during the establishment and early development of the UN (1941–49; 1953–57); his close identification with Stalin caused him to fall from favour during the Khrushchev years.

Nasser, Gammal Abdel (1918–70):   Nationalist army officer who led Egypt from 1952 until his death in 1970; nationalized the Suez Canal in 1956, thus leading indirectly to the establishment of UNEF; leading figure in 1967 combined Arab attack on Israel (the 'Six-Day War')

Nixon, Richard (1913–94):   US president (Republican) 1969–74; although fundamentally conservative in foreign policy (as regards, for example, American policy in Southeast Asia), he presided over the development of détente – including rapprochement with communist China – in tandem with his secretary of state Henry Kissinger; resigned after the Watergate scandal in 1974.

O'Brien, Conor Cruise (1917–):   Irish diplomat, politician and writer; seconded from the Irish foreign service to act as UN representative in Katanga in 1961 where he ordered UN forces to take action against foreign military personnel supporting secession; the ensuing crisis led indirectly to the death of Hammarskjöld.

Pearson, Lester (1897–1972):   Canadian foreign minister 1948–57 closely associated with Canada's 'middle power' role in the UN; his General Assembly initiative during the Suez crisis in 1956 led to the creation of UNEF; Nobel Peace Prize winner; prime minister of Canada 1963–68.

Pérez de Cuéllar, Javier (1920–):   Peruvian secretary-general of UN 1982–92; the end of his term of office saw the beginning of the UN's post-cold war peacekeeping after the dormant period of the late 1970s and 1980s.

Rabin, Yitzhak (1922–95):   Israeli (Labour) prime minister from 1974 to 1977 and from 1992 until his murder by a Jewish extremist; negotiated with Henry Kissinger in 1974 over the formation of UNDOF in the Golan Heights and was involved in the Israel–Egypt talks which led eventually to the Camp David agreement.

Reagan, Ronald (1911–):   US president (Republican) 1980–88; presided over the worst years of the 'second' cold war in the 1980s; his administration pursued a distinctly conservative foreign policy and was frequently hostile to the UN as an institution.

Roosevelt, Franklin D. (1882–1945):   US president (Democrat) for three terms from 1933 until his death in 1945; his 'New Deal' policies helped alleviate the worst effects of the depression in the 1930s; took America into the Second World War and became the chief architect of the UN and strong advocate of collective security; died on the eve of the San Francisco conference at which his efforts came to fruition.

Sadat, Anwar (1918–81):   President of Egypt from 1970 until his assassination by opposition elements in the Egyptian army in 1981; leading actor in the Arab attack on Israel in 1973 and then subsequently in the peace process which led to the Camp David agreement between Egypt and Israel in 1978.

Stalin, Joseph (1879–1953):   Leader of the Soviet Union after the death of Lenin in 1923; over the following thirty years he presided over massive repression at home; led the Soviet Union to (a costly) victory in the Second World War; co-operated with Roosevelt and Churchill in the planning of the UN in 1944–45 to ensure that the USSR was not isolated in post-war international relations; gave encouragement to (if not order for) North Korea's invasion of the South in 1950.

Stettinius, Edward (1900–49):   US secretary of state under Truman; previously chairman and participant at the Dumbarton Oaks conference in 1944.

Stevenson, Adlai (1900–65):   US representative at the UN under Kennedy and Johnson; associated with a 'liberal' period in American UN policy; previously Democratic candidate in the presidential elections of 1952 and 1956.

Sukarno, Ahmed (1901–70):   First president of Indonesia 1945–67; prominent internationally in the development of the Non-Aligned Movement while pursuing an aggressively nationalist foreign policy in the Asia-Pacific region; succeeded in annexing West New Guinea with the help of a UN temporary executive and peacekeeping force (UNTEA/UNSF) in 1962–63.

Syngman Rhee (1875–1965):   First president of South Korea 1945–60; pro-western, right-wing nationalist; in office during the Korean War.

Truman, Harry S. (1884–1972):   US president (Democrat) 1945–53; succeeded Roosevelt at key stage in the formation of the UN; in office during the Korean War.

Tshombe, Moise (1919–69):   Leader of the Congo province of Katanga which attempted to secede (with foreign encouragement and help) from the new state; after UN-led extinction of Katangese secession became prominent for a short time in Congolese national politics.

U Thant (1909–74):   Burmese secretary-general of the UN who took over after the death of Hammarskjöld in September 1961 and remained in office until 1972; successfully managed the financial-constitutional (Article 19) crisis of 1964; presided over the formation of UNFICYP.

Waldheim, Kurt (1918–):   Austrian secretary-general of the UN 1972–82; in office during the formation of UNEF II and UNDOF in 1973–74 and of UNIFIL in 1978; his term coincided with the high point of superpower détente; later president of Austria despite controversy surrounding 'hidden' past in wartime German army.

Wilson, Woodrow (1856–1924):   US president (Democrat) 1913–21; strong moral voice at the Treaty of Versailles following the First World War; architect of the League of Nations and early advocate of collective security; vision not shared by US Congress, which rejected US participation in the League.

Yeltsin, Boris (1931–):   Russian president who succeeded Gorbachev at the end of 1991 after the break-up of the Soviet Union; co-operated with the west in the UN during the Gulf War; more hostile to western positions on the former Yugoslavia.

UN OPERATIONS, 1948–1998: BASIC DATA

UNITED NATIONS TRUCE SUPERVISION ORGANIZATION (UNTSO)
Location:	Israeli border/Palestine
Date formed:	June 1948
Strength:	180 (mid–1990s)
Function:	Observation of cease-fires and truces between Israel and Arab states and assistance to other UN peacekeeping operations in the region.

UNITED NATIONS MILITARY OBSERVER GROUP IN INDIA AND PAKISTAN (UNMOGIP)
Location:	India–Pakistan cease-fire line in Kashmir
Date formed:	January 1949
Strength:	45 (mid-1990s)
Function:	To observe cease-fire between India and Pakistan following war over disputed territory in 1948.

UNITED NATIONS EMERGENCY FORCE (UNEF)
Location:	Suez Canal and Sinai peninsula
Date formed:	November 1956
Strength:	6,000
Function:	To supervise cessation of hostilities between Israel and Egypt and, initially, to supervise withdrawal of Anglo-French forces from Canal Zone. Withdrawn at the request of Egypt in May 1967.

UNITED NATIONS OBSERVATION GROUP IN LEBANON (UNOGIL)
Location:	Lebanese-Syrian border
Date formed:	June 1958
Strength:	600
Function:	To prevent infiltration into Lebanon of hostile elements. Withdrawn in December 1958.

UNITED NATIONS OPERATION IN CONGO (ONUC)

Location: Republic of Congo (previously Belgian Congo;
                    subsequently Zaire then Democratic Republic of Congo)
Date formed: July 1960
Strength: 20,000
Function: Initially to supervise the withdrawal of Belgian forces; later
                    to provide stability in, and ensure the territorial integrity
                    of, the new state. Withdrawn in June 1964.

UNITED NATIONS SECURITY FORCE IN WEST NEW GUINEA (UNSF)

Location: Dutch New Guinea/Indonesian province of Irian Jaya
Date formed: October 1962
Strength: 1,600
Function: To provide security for the territory during the administra-
                    tion of the UN Temporary Executive Authority (UNTEA).
                    UNTEA was the interim government during the transfer of
                    power in West New Guinea from the Netherlands to
                    Indonesia. Mission completed in April 1963.

UNITED NATIONS YEMEN OBSERVATION MISSION (UNYOM)

Location: Yemen
Date formed: July 1963
Strength: 200
Function: To supervise mutual disengagement from Yemen civil war
                    of Saudi Arabia and United Arab Republic (Egypt).
                    Withdrawn in September 1964.

UNITED NATIONS FORCE IN CYPRUS (UNFICYP)

Location: Cyprus
Date formed: March 1964
Strength: 1,200 (mid-1990s)
Function: To prevent fighting between Greek and Turkish Cypriot
                    communities. After 1974 Turkish invasion, to supervise
                    cease-fire line between Turkish/Turkish Cypriot forces and
                    Greek Cypriot forces.

UNITED NATIONS INDIA–PAKISTAN OBSERVATION MISSION (UNIPOM)

Location: India–Pakistan border west of Kashmir
Date formed: September 1965
Strength: 100
Function: To supervise cease-fire following 1965 India–Pakistan war.
                    Withdrawn in March 1966.

SECOND UNITED NATIONS EMERGENCY FORCE (UNEF II)

Location:	Suez Canal area and Sinai peninsula
Date formed:	October 1973
Strength:	7,000
Function:	To supervise Israeli–Egyptian cease-fire following 1973 war and to provide a buffer between disengaging forces. Mandate terminated at Soviet insistence in July 1979.

UNITED NATIONS DISENGAGEMENT OBSERVERVATION FORCE (UNDOF)

Location:	Golan Heights (Israeli–Syrian border)
Date formed:	June 1974
Strength:	1,000 (mid-1990s)
Function:	To supervise disengagement of Israeli and Syrian forces following 1973 war and to provide a buffer between forces.

UNITED NATIONS INTERIM FORCE IN LEBANON (UNIFIL)

Location:	Southern Lebanon
Date formed:	March 1978
Strength:	4,600 (mid-1990s)
Function:	To oversee Israeli withdrawal from Lebanon following 1978 invasion and assist return of Lebanese government authority to southern Lebanon.

UNITED NATIONS GOOD OFFICES MISSION IN AFGHANISTAN AND PAKISTAN (UNGOMAP)

Location:	Afghanistan and Pakistan
Date formed:	May 1988
Strength:	50
Function:	To supervise peace agreement following withdrawal of Soviet forces from Afghanistan. Mission completed March 1990.

UNITED NATIONS IRAN–IRAQ MILITARY OBSERVER GROUP (UNIIMOG)

Location:	Iran and Iraq
Date formed:	August 1988
Strength:	400
Function:	To supervise Iran–Iraq cease-fire following the peace agreement to end the war in course since 1980. Mission completed February 1991.

FIRST UNITED NATIONS ANGOLA VERIFICATION MISSION (UNAVEM I)

Location:	Angola
Date formed:	January 1989
Strength:	70
Function:	To supervise withdrawal of Cuban forces from Angola. Mission successfully completed in May 1991 ahead of schedule.

UNITED NATIONS TRANSITION ASSISTANCE GROUP (UNTAG)

Location:	Namibia
Date formed:	April 1989
Strength:	8,000
Function:	To provide security and administrative support during Namibia's transition to independence from South Africa. Mission completed March 1990.

UNITED NATIONS OBSERVER GROUP IN CENTRAL AMERICA (ONUCA)

Location:	Costa Rica, El Salvador, Guatemala, Honduras, Nicaragua
Date formed:	December 1989
Strength:	1,000
Function:	To supervise regional agreement to prevent cross-border movement of irregular forces and arms, in particular from and to Nicaragua. Withdrawn January 1992.

UNITED NATIONS IRAQ–KUWAIT OBSERVATION MISSION (UNIKOM)

Location:	Iraq–Kuwait border
Date formed:	April 1991
Strength:	1,200 (mid-1990s)
Function:	To monitor demilitarized zone on Iraq–Kuwait border following the expulsion of Iraqi forces from Kuwait after Operation Desert Storm.

UNITED NATIONS MISSION FOR THE REFERENDUM IN WESTERN SAHARA (MINURSO)

Location:	Western Sahara
Date formed:	April 1991
Strength:	2,500
Function:	Following agreement between Morocco and Polisario Front, to supervise disengagement of both sides' forces and to prepare elections on the future of the territory.

SECOND UNITED NATIONS ANGOLA VERIFICATION MISSION (UNAVEM II)

Location:	Angola
Date formed:	May 1991
Strength:	350
Function:	To verify cease-fire between Angolan government and UNITA guerrillas, and to monitor national elections. Withdrawn February 1995.

UNITED NATIONS OBSERVATION MISSION IN EL SALVADOR (ONUSAL)

Location:	El Salvador
Date formed:	July 1991
Strength:	1,000
Function:	To verify cease-fire between El Salvador government and leftist guerrillas, and to supervise national elections. Withdrawn April 1995.

UNITED NATIONS PROTECTION FORCE (UNPROFOR)

Location:	Bosnia, Croatia, Serbia, Montenegro
Date formed:	February 1992
Strength:	39,000
Function:	First deployed in Croatia and then most notably in Bosnia to secure UN 'protected areas', provide security for humanitarian aid and monitor UN-declared air exclusion zones. Wound up March 1995 after the Dayton peace agreement and replaced with NATO-led 'Implementation Force'.

UNITED NATIONS TRANSITIONAL AUTHORITY IN CAMBODIA (UNTAC)

Location:	Cambodia
Date formed:	March 1992
Strength:	22,000
Function:	To supervise implementation of 1991 peace agreement in Cambodia; to provide an interim authority and to prepare and administer national elections. Mission completed in September 1993.

UNITED NATIONS OPERATION IN SOMALIA (UNOSOM)/UNIFIED TASK FORCE (UNITAF)

Location:	Somalia
Date formed:	April/December 1992
Strength:	28,000
Function:	To restore peace and stability by ending factional fighting in Somalia and to secure the distribution of humanitarian aid. Withdrawn March 1995.

UNITED NATIONS OPERATION IN MOZAMBIQUE (ONUMOZ)

Location:	Mozambique
Date formed:	December 1992
Strength:	7,000
Function:	To assist in the implementation of the peace agreement between Mozambican government and Renamo guerrillas; to administer and supervise national elections. Mission completed December 1994.

UNITED NATIONS OBSERVER MISSION UGANDA–RWANDA (UNOMUR)

Location:	Uganda–Rwanda border
Date formed:	June 1993
Strength:	80
Function:	To ensure no military forces or material permitted to cross Uganda–Rwanda border. Withdrawn September 1994.

UNITED NATIONS OBSERVER MISSION IN GEORGIA (UNOMIG)

Location:	Georgia (former Soviet Union)
Date formed:	August 1993
Strength:	140
Function:	Initially, to verify peace agreement between government of Georgia and Abkhaz separatists; later, to monitor operation of Commonwealth of Independent States (of the former Soviet Union) peacekeeping force in Georgia.

UNITED NATIONS OBSERVER MISSION IN LIBERIA (UNOMIL)

Location:	Liberia
Date formed:	September 1993
Strength:	160
Function:	To support and monitor the peacekeeping efforts of the Economic Community of West African States (ECOWAS) in Liberia after the end of the civil war in 1993.

UNITED NATIONS MISSION IN HAITI (UNMIH)

Location:	Haiti
Date formed:	September 1993
Strength:	1,200 (mid-1990s)
Function:	Originally, to train and modernize Haitian security forces. After the 1994 US intervention UNMIH assisted the new government in preparation of elections.

UNITED NATIONS ASSISTANCE MISSION FOR RWANDA (UNAMIR)

Location:	Rwanda
Date formed:	October 1993
Strength:	5,500
Function:	Originally, to implement peace agreement between Rwanda government and rebel forces. Overtaken by genocide and subsequent revolution in Rwanda in mid-1994. Given a renewed humanitarian mandate in aftermath of this. Withdrawn March 1996.

UNITED NATIONS MISSION OF OBSERVERS IN TAJIKISTAN (UNMOT)

Location:	Tajikistan
Date formed:	December 1994
Strength:	45
Function:	To monitor cease-fire on Tajik–Afghan border; to liaise with Organization for Security and Co-operation in Europe (OSCE) mission and to monitor Commonwealth of Independent States peacekeeping force.

THIRD UNITED NATIONS VERIFICATION MISSION IN ANGOLA (UNAVEM III)

Location:	Angola
Date formed:	February 1995
Strength:	7,000
Function:	To supervise implementation of Lusaka peace agreement of 1994 after resumption of civil war between government forces and UNITA in 1992. Replaced by new UN observer mission June 1997.

UNITED NATIONS OBSERVATION MISSION IN ANGOLA (MONUA)

Location:	Angola
Date formed:	June 1997
Strength:	2,500
Function:	To continue efforts of UNAVEM III to complete the outstanding aspects of the Lusaka peace agreement.

CHRONOLOGY

1941 August: Roosevelt and Churchill meet and agree 'Atlantic Charter'.

1943 November: Tehran Conference – Roosevelt outlines his big power 'policemen' concept for post-war security.

1944 August: Dumbarton Oaks conference – American, Soviet, British and Chinese representatives agree outline for a new international organization based on the principle of collective security.

1945 February: Yalta conference – the plan for the UN is discussed by Roosevelt, Stalin and Churchill.

     April: Death of Roosevelt – succeeded by Truman. San Francisco conference to finalize preparations for the new organization. Attended by the 'big five' (US, USSR, UK, France and China) and fifty other anti-Axis states.

     May: Germany surrenders.

     August: Japan surrenders.

1946 February: UN's first secretary-general, Trygve Lie of Norway, takes office.

1948 April: Berlin crisis.

     May: British Mandate ends in Palestine – State of Israel declared and war breaks out.

     June: United Nations Truce Supervision Organization (UNTSO) established for Palestine.

     September: UN Mediator for Palestine, Count Bernadotte, murdered.

1949	January:	United Nations Military Observer Group in India and Pakistan (UNMOGIP) established.
1950	June:	North Korea invades the South across 38th parallel. Security Council resolution (S/RES/82) demands its withdrawal (Soviet Union absent from Security Council). United States mobilizes forces in support of the South.
	July:	Security Council resolution (S/RES/84) authorizes American-led 'Unified Command' to confront North Korean invaders.
	August:	Soviet delegation returns to Security Council.
	September:	Inchon landing by 'UN' forces turns tide and forces North Korea back towards 38th parallel.
	October:	'UN' forces cross northwards over 38th parallel.
	November:	'Uniting for Peace' resolution passed by General Assembly. Communist Chinese cross into North Korea to confront western forces.
1951	January:	Chinese and North Korean forces push south again across 38th parallel.
	April:	Truman dismisses General MacArthur from command of western forces in Korea.
	June:	Western forces push northwards in Korea again. Cease-fire talks proposed.
1953	January:	Eisenhower inaugurated as US president in succession to Truman.
	March:	Death of Stalin – succeeded by 'collective leadership' including Nikita Khrushchev.
	April:	Trygve Lie succeeded as UN secretary-general by Dag Hammarskjöld of Sweden.
	July:	Armistice signed in Korea.
1956	July:	Nasser nationalizes the Suez Canal.
	October:	Hungarian uprising suppressed by Russians. Israeli attack on Egypt followed by Anglo-French 'ultimatum' and air-raids on Suez Canal Zone. US draft resolution in Security Council calling for Israeli withdrawal (S/3710) vetoed by Britain and France.
	November:	Anglo-French forces invade Suez. General Assembly resolution establishes United Nations Emergency Force (UNEF) for Suez.

1958	February:	Egypt and Syria declare themselves unified as the 'United Arab Republic'.
	October:	Hammarskjöld produces 'Summary Study' on lessons of Suez.
	June:	United Nations Observation Group in Lebanon (UNOGIL) formed in response to Lebanese government claims of Syrian infiltration.
	July:	US troops landed in Lebanon.
	December:	Lebanon crisis recedes – UNOGIL withdrawn.
1960	June:	Independence of Congo from Belgium.
	July:	Congolese army mutinies – Belgian paratroops intervene.
		Congolese prime minister (Lumumba) and president (Kasavubu) seek UN assistance.
		Katanga announces secession from Congo.
		Security Council resolution (S/RES/143) establishes United Nations Operation in Congo (ONUC).
	September:	Congolese government crisis – Kasavubu dismisses Lumumba and *vice versa*. UN orders closure of airports and radio station.
		Congolese army commander Mobutu announces coup and allies himself with Kasavubu. Lumumba under UN protection.
		Khrushchev denounces 'pro-western' stance of ONUC in Security Council – calls for *troika* to replace office of secretary-general.
	November:	General Assembly recognizes Kasavubu–Mobutu faction as legitimate government of Congo.
		Lumumba leaves UN protection and is captured by Mobutu's forces.
1961	January:	Lumumba murdered after being transferred by his captors to Katanga.
		John F. Kennedy inaugurated as US president.
	February:	Security Council resolution (S/RES/161) authorizes ONUC to use force if necessary to prevent civil war in Congo.
	August–September:	Unsuccessful UN military operations against Katanga.
	September:	Death of Hammarskjöld en route to meet Katangese leaders in Northern Rhodesia. Succeeded as secretary-general by U Thant of Burma.
1962	July:	Advisory Opinion of International Court of Justice that peacekeeping is a 'normal' expense of the UN.

	October:	United Nations Temporary Executive Authority/ Security Force (UNTEA/UNSF) created for West New Guinea.
		Cuban missile crisis.
1963	January:	Katangese secession formally ended in face of mounting UN military pressure.
	May:	UNTEA/UNSF completes mission in West New Guinea.
	July:	United Nations Yemen Observation Mission (UNYOM) deployed.
	August:	Partial Nuclear Test Ban Treaty signed in Moscow by US, USSR and Britain.
	November:	Kennedy assassinated – Lyndon Johnson becomes US president.
1964	March:	United Nations Force in Cyprus (UNFICYP) formed by Security Council resolution (S/RES/186) in response to widespread inter-communal violence.
	June:	Withdrawal of ONUC from Congo.
	September:	UNYOM completes mission in Yemen.
	September– December:	'Article 19 crisis' over General Assembly voting rights.
	October:	Khrushchev deposed. Replaced by new leadership including Leonid Brezhnev.
1965	September:	United Nations India–Pakistan Observation Mission (UNIPOM) established.
1966	March:	UNIPOM withdrawn from India–Pakistan border.
1967	May:	UNEF withdrawn from Suez at request of Egypt.
	June:	'Six Day War' between Israel and Arabs.
	November:	UNFICYP responds to sharp deterioration in Cyprus situation.
1968	January– February:	Vietnam war intensifies with 'Tet Offensive' by Vietcong.
	August:	Russian tanks suppress reformist movement in Czechoslovakia.
1969	January:	Richard Nixon sworn in as US president.
1971	October:	Communist China replaces Formosa/Taiwan in the 'China seat' at the UN following rapprochement between Washington and Beijing.

1972	January:	Kurt Waldheim of Austria becomes UN secretary-general.
	May:	Nixon and Brezhnev sign Strategic Arms Limitation Treaty (SALT) in Moscow.
1973	October:	War in the Middle East. US and USSR co-operate in orchestrating UN response.
		Second United Nations Emergency Force (UNEF II) deployed between Israeli and Egyptian armies in Sinai.
1974	June:	United Nations Disengagement Observation Force (UNDOF) deployed between Israeli and Syrian armies in Golan Heights.
	July–August:	Coup attempt in Cyprus by right-wing Greek Cypriots provokes Turkish invasion. UNFICYP interposed between warring sides. Cyprus effectively partitioned.
	August:	Nixon forced to resign following Watergate scandal. Gerald Ford becomes president.
1975	April:	Saigon falls to North Vietnamese forces. Final American withdrawal from South Vietnam.
		Civil war breaks out in Lebanon.
	November:	Portugal withdraws from Angola – civil war between US- and Soviet-backed factions. Cuban troops intervene in support of Marxist government.
1976	June:	Syria moves against Palestinians in Lebanon.
1977	January:	Jimmy Carter sworn in as US president.
1978	March:	Israeli invasion of Lebanon. Security Council approves (S/RES/426) formation of United Nations Interim Force in Lebanon (UNIFIL).
	September:	Camp David agreement between Israel and Egypt.
1979	January:	Shah of Iran deposed. Anti-western Islamist regime installed.
	June:	Second Strategic Arms Limitation Treaty (SALT-2) signed by Carter and Brezhnev in Vienna.
	July:	UNEF II withdrawn from Sinai at the insistence of the Soviet Union.
	December:	Soviet invasion of Afghanistan.
1981	January:	Ronald Reagan sworn in as US president.

1982	January:	Javier Pérez de Cuéllar of Peru replaces Kurt Waldheim as UN secretary-general.
	June:	Israel invades Lebanon again. UNIFIL brushed aside.
	August:	Non-UN Multinational Force (MNF) established to oversee withdrawal of Palestinians from Beirut and act as buffer between Israeli and Syrian forces.
	November:	Brezhnev dies, succeeded by Yuri Andropov.
1983	October:	300 US and French troops of the MNF in Lebanon killed in bomb attacks. Force withdrawn.
1984	February:	Andropov dies, succeeded as Soviet leader by Konstantin Chernenko.
1985	March:	Chernenko dies, succeeded by Mikhail Gorbachev.
1987	December:	Strategic Arms Reduction Treaty (START) signed by Reagan and Gorbachev in Washington.
1988	April:	United Nations Good Offices Mission in Afghanistan and Pakistan (UNGOMAP) established.
	August:	United Nations Iran–Iraq Military Observer Group (UNIIMOG) formed.
1989	January:	George Bush sworn in as US president. First United Nations Angola Verification Mission (UNAVEM I) formed.
	April:	United Nations Transition Assistance Group (UNTAG) for Namibia established.
	November:	Berlin Wall comes down. United Nations Observer Group in Central America (ONUCA) formed.
1990	March:	UNTAG completes mission in Namibia. UNGOMAP completes mission in Afghanistan and Pakistan.
	August:	Iraq invades Kuwait.
	October:	Unification of Germany.
	November:	Security Council resolution (S/RES/678) authorizes formation of military coalition against Iraq.
1991	January:	Operation Desert Storm begins against Iraq.
	February:	UNIIMOG completes mission on Iran–Iraq border.
	April:	United Nations Iraq–Kuwait Observation Mission (UNIKOM) formed.

	United Nations Mission for the Referendum in Western Sahara (MINURSO) formed.
June:	UNAVEM I completes mission in Angola ahead of schedule.
	Second Angola Verification Mission (UNAVEM II) formed.
July:	United Nations Observation Mission in El Salvador (ONUSAL) formed.
September:	Soviet Union formally dissolved. Commonwealth of Independent States (CIS) succeeds it.
December:	Gorbachev resigns as president of CIS and hands power to Russian president Boris Yeltsin.

1992	January:	Boutros Boutros-Ghali of Egypt replaces Pérez de Cuéllar as UN secretary-general.
		ONUCA completes mission in Central America.
	March:	United Nations Protection Force (UNPROFOR) for former Yugoslavia established.
		United Nations Transitional Authority in Cambodia (UNTAC) formed.
	April:	United Nations Operation in Somalia (UNOSOM) established.
	June:	Boutros-Ghali publishes *An Agenda for Peace*.
	December:	United Nations Operation in Mozambique (ONU-MOZ) established.
		American-led Unified Task Force in Somalia (UNITAF) deployed.

1993	January:	Bill Clinton sworn in as US president.
	May:	UNITAF withdrawn from Somalia. Replaced by UNOSOM II.
	June:	United Nations Observer Mission Uganda–Rwanda (UNOMUR) formed.
	August:	United Nations Observer Mission in Georgia (UNOMIG) formed.
	September:	United Nations Observer Mission in Liberia (UNOMIL) established.
		United Nations Mission in Haiti (UNMIH) formed.
	October:	United Nations Assistance Mission for Rwanda (UNAMIR) established.

1994	April:	Genocide begins in Rwanda. UN troops withdrawn.
	September:	UNOMUR withdrawn from Uganda–Rwanda border.
	December:	ONUMOZ completes mission in Mozambique.
		United Nations Mission of Observers in Tajikistan (UNMOT) formed.

1995 February: UNAVEM II wound-up in Angola.
                   Third United Nations Angola Verification Mission
                       (UNAVEM III) formed.
      March: UNOSOM II withdraws from Somalia.
      April: ONUSAL completes mission in El Salvador.
      August: NATO-led 'Operation Deliberate Force' mounted
                       against Bosnian Serbs.
      November: Dayton Agreement on Bosnia signed.
      December: UNPROFOR wound down in Bosnia; replaced by
                       NATO Implementation Force (I–FOR).

1996 October: UNAMIR withdrawn from Rwanda.

1997 January: Kofi Annan of Ghana replaces Boutros-Ghali as UN
                       secretary-general.
      May: Mobutu overthrown in Zaire (former Congo).
      June: UNAVEM III wound-up in Angola; replaced by United
                       Nations Angola Observation Mission (MONUA).

BIBLIOGRAPHY

PRIMARY SOURCES

1   Anstee, M., *Orphan of the Cold War: The Inside Story of the Collapse of the Angolan Peace Process, 1992–93* (London: Macmillan, 1996).

2   Boutros-Ghali, B., *An Agenda for Peace* (New York: UN, 1982).

3   Burns, E.L.M., *Between Arab and Israeli* (London: Harrap, 1962).

4   Dayal, R., *Mission for Hammarskjöld: The Congo Crisis* (Oxford: Oxford University Press, 1976).

5   Dobrynin, A.F., *In Confidence: Moscow's Ambassador to America's Six Cold War Presidents* (New York: Times Books, 1995).

6   Gromyko, A.A., *Memories* (London, Hutchinson, 1989).

7   Hammarskjöld, D., *Markings* (London: Faber & Faber, 1964).

8   Higgins, R., *United Nations Peacekeeping 1946–67: Documents and Commentary* Vol. 1 *The Middle East* (Oxford: Oxford University Press, 1969).

9   Higgins, R., *United Nations Peacekeeping 1946–67: Documents and Commentary* Vol. 2 *Asia* (Oxford: Oxford University Press, 1970).

10   Higgins, R., *United Nations Peacekeeping 1946–67: Documents and Commentary* Vol. 3 *Africa* (Oxford: Oxford University Press, 1980).

11   Higgins, R., *United Nations Peacekeeping: Documents and Commentary 1946–79* Vol. 4 *The Middle East* (Oxford: Oxford University Press, 1981).

12   Horn, Carl von, *Soldiering for Peace* (London: Cassell, 1966).

13   Kissinger, H., *Years of Upheaval* (London: Weidenfeld & Nicolson, 1982).

14   Khrushchev, N., *Khrushchev Remembers: The Last Testament*, ed. Strobe Talbot (London: André Deutsch, 1974).

15   Lie, T., *In the Cause of Peace* (New York: Macmillan, 1954).

16   O'Brien, C.C., *To Katanga and Back* (London: Huchinson, 1962).

17   Pearson, L., *Memoirs Vol. 2 1948–1957* (Toronto: University of Toronto Press, 1973).

18   Rikyhe, I.J., *The Theory and Practice of Peacekeeping* (London: Hurst, 1984).

19   U Thant, *View from the UN* (New York: Doubleday, 1978).
20   United Nations, *The Blue Helmets: A Review of UN Peacekeeping* (New York: UN 1990).
21   United Nations Documents: General Assembly (A/ series); Security Council (S/ series).
22   Urquhart, B., *A Life in Peace and War* (London: Weidenfeld & Nicolson, 1987).
23   Waldheim, K., *In the Eye of the Storm* (London: Weidenfeld & Nicolson, 1985).

THE COLD WAR AND INTERNATIONAL POLITICS

24   Ambrose, S., *Rise to Globalism: American Foreign Policy since 1938* (Harmondsworth: Penguin, 1988).
25   Ashton, S.R., *In Search of Détente: The Politics of East–West Relations since 1945* (London: Macmillan, 1989).
26   Bartlett, C.J., *The Global Conflict: The International Rivalry of the Great Powers 1880–1990* (London: Longman, 1994).
27   Bell, C., *The Diplomacy of Détente: The Kissinger Era* (London: Martin Robertson, 1977).
28   Beschloss, M., *Kennedy and Khrushchev: The Crisis Years, 1960–1963* (London: Faber & Faber, 1991).
29   Calvocoressi, P., *World Politics since 1945* (London: Longman, 1996).
30   Crockatt, R., *The Fifty Years War: The United States and the Soviet Union in World Politics 1941–1991* (London: Routledge, 1994).
31   Divine, R., *Foreign Policy and US Presidential Elections, 1940–1948* (New York: New Viewpoints, 1974).
32   Dunrabbin, J.P.D., *The Cold War: The Great Powers and their Allies* (London: Longman, 1994).
33   Dunrabbin, J.P.D., *The Post-Imperial Age: The Great Powers and the Wider World* (London: Longman, 1994).
34   Gaddis, J.L., *The United States and the Origins of the Cold War, 1941–47* (New York: Columbia University Press, 1972).
35   Gaddis, J.L., *We Know Now: Rethinking Cold War History* (Oxford: Clarendon Press, 1997).
36   Garthoff, R., *Détente and Confrontation: American-Soviet Relations, Nixon to Reagan* (Washington DC: Brookings Institute, 1985).
37   Halliday, F., *The Making of the Second Cold War* (London: Verso, 1987).
38   Hastings, M., *The Korean War* (London: Michael Joseph, 1988).
39   Horowitz, D., *From Yalta to Vietnam* (Harmondsworth: Penguin, 1967).
40   Hoskyns, C., *The Congo since Independence, January 1960 – December 1961* (Oxford: Oxford University Press, 1965).
41   Isaacson, W., *Kissinger: A Biography* (London: Faber & Faber, 1992).
42   Kedourie, E., *Politics in the Middle East* (Oxford: Oxford University Press, 1992).

43   Kyle, K., *Suez* (London: Weidenfeld & Nicolson, 1991).

44   Leffler, M.P. and Painter, D.S., *The Origins of the Cold War: An International History* (London: Routledge, 1994).

45   Litwak, R., *Détente and the Nixon Doctrine: American Foreign Policy and the Pursuit of Stability, 1969–1976* (Cambridge: Cambridge University Press, 1986).

46   Louis, W.R. and Owen, R., *Suez 1956: The Crisis and its Consequences* (Oxford: Clarendon Press, 1989).

47   Louis, W.R., Stookry, R.W. and Wilson, R., *The End of the Palestine Mandate* (London: Tauris, 1986).

48   Mahoney, R., *JFK: Ordeal in Africa* (Oxford: Oxford University Press, 1983).

49   McCauley, M., *The Khrushchev Era, 1953–64* (London: Longman, 1995).

50   McWilliams, W.C. and Piotrowski, H., *The World since 1945: A History of International Relations* (London: Rienner, 1997).

51   Ovendale, R., *Britain, the United States and the End of the Palestine Mandate 1942–48* (London: Royal Historical Society, 1989)

52   Ovendale, R., *The Origins of the Arab-Israeli Wars* (London: Longman, 1992).

53   Paige, G.D., *The Korean Decision* (New York: Collier Macmillan, 1968).

54   Pipes, R., *US-Soviet Relations in the Era of Détente* (Boulder CO: Westview, 1981).

55   Powaski, R.E., *The Cold War: The United States and the Soviet Union, 1917–1991* (Oxford: Oxford University Press, 1997).

56   Quandt, W.R., *Camp David: Peacemaking and Politics* (Washington DC: Brookings Institute, 1986).

57   Rees, D., *The Age of Containment: The Cold War 1945–65* (London: Macmillan, 1967).

58   Stevenson, R.W., *The Rise and Fall of Détente: Relaxations of Tension in US-Soviet Relations, 1953–84* (London: Macmillan, 1985).

59   Thomas, H., *The Suez Affair* (London: Weidenfeld & Nicholson, 1967).

60   Vadney, T.E., *The World since 1945* (Harmondsworth: Penguin, 1992).

61   Walker, M., *The Cold War and the Making of the Modern World* (London: Fourth Estate, 1993).

62   Weissman, S.R., *American Foreign Policy in the Congo, 1960–64* (Ithaca NY: Cornell University Press, 1974).

63   Whelan, R., *Drawing the Line: The Korean War, 1950–1953* (Boston: Little Brown, 1990).

64   Young, J.W., *Longman Companion to Cold War and Détente 1941–91* (London: Longman, 1993).

THE UNITED NATIONS AND INTERNATIONAL ORGANIZATION

65   Archer, C., *International Organizations* (London: Routledge, 1992).

66   Armstrong, D., *The Rise of the International Organization: A Short History* (London: Macmillan, 1982).

67   Armstrong, D. *et al.*, *From Versailles to Maastricht: International Organization in the 20th Century* (London: Macmillan,1996).

68   Baehr, P.R. and Gordenker, L., *The United Nations in the 1990s* (New York: St Martin's Press, 1994).

69   Bailey, S.D., *The Procedure of the UN Security Council* (Oxford: Clarendon Press, 1988).

70   Bailey, S.D., *The General Assembly of the United Nations* (London: Pall Mall, 1964).

71   Bailey, S.D., *The United Nations: A Concise Political Guide* (London: Macmillan, 1994).

72   Bennett, A.L., *International Organization: Principles and Issues* (5th edn, Englewood Cliffs NJ: Prentice Hall, 1991).

73   Berridge, G., *Return to the UN: UN Diplomacy in Regional Conflicts* (London: Macmillan, 1990).

74   Bertrand, M., 'The historical development of efforts to reform the UN' in Roberts, A. and Kingsbury, B. (eds), *United Nations, Divided World* (Oxford, Oxford University Press, 1993), pp. 420–36.

75   Bourantonis, D. (ed.), *The United Nations in the New World Order: The World Organization at Fifty* (London: Macmillan, 1995).

76   Boyd, A., *Fifteen Men on a Powder Keg: A History of the UN Security Council* (London: Methuen, 1971).

77   Claude, I.L., *The Changing United Nations* (New York: Random House, 1967).

78   Claude, I.L., *Swords into Plowshares* (London: McGraw Hill, 1984).

79   Goodrich, L.M. *et al.*, *Charter of the United Nations: Commentary and Documents* (New York: Columbia University Press, 1969).

80   Goodrich, L.M., *The United Nations in a Changing World* (New York: Columbia University Press, 1974).

81   Hiscocks, R., *The Security Council: A Study in Adolescence* (London: Longman, 1973).

82   James, A., 'The United Nations' in Armstrong, D. and Goldstein, E. (eds), *The End of the Cold War* (London: Frank Cass, 1990), pp. 182–95.

83   Luard, E., *A History of the United Nations: Vol. I The Years of Western Domination, 1945–55* (London: Macmillan, 1982).

84   Luard, E., *A History of the United Nations: Vol. II The Age of Decolonization, 1955–65* (London: Macmillan, 1989).

85   Luard, E. and Heater, D., *The United Nations: How it Works and What it Does* (2nd edn, London: Macmillan, 1994).

86   Nicholas, H.G., *The United Nations as a Political Institution* (Oxford: Oxford University Press, 1971).

87   Northedge, F.S., *The League of Nations: Its Life and Times, 1920–1946* (Leicester: Leicester University Press, 1985).
88   Peterson, M.J., *The General Assembly in World Politics* (Boston: Unwin Hyman, 1986).
89   Rovine, A., *The First Fifty Years of the Secretary-General in World Politics, 1920–1970* (Leyden: Sijthoff, 1970).
90   Russell, R.B., *A History of the United Nations Charter* (Washington DC: Brookings Institute, 1958).
91   Shaw, M.N., *International Law* (Cambridge: Cambridge University Press, 1995).
92   Simons, G., *The United Nations: A Chronology of Conflict* (London: Macmillan, 1994).
93   Simons, G., *UN Malaise: Power, Problems and Realpolitik* (London: Macmillan, 1995).
94   Stoessinger, J.G., *The United Nations and the Superpowers* (New York: Random House, 1977).
95   Stoessinger, J.G. *et al.*, *Financing the United Nations System* (Washington DC: Brookings Institute, 1964).
96   Urquhart, B., *Hammarskjöld* (London: Bodley Head, 1973).
97   Walters, F.P., *A History of the League of Nations* (Oxford: Oxford University Press, 1960).
98   Whittaker, D.J., *The United Nations in Action* (London: UCL Press, 1995).
99   Whittaker, D.J., *United Nations in the Contemporary World* (London: Routledge, 1997).
100   Yoder, A., *The Evolution of the United Nations System* (London: Taylor & Francis, 1997).
101   Zacher, M.W., *Dag Hammarskjöld's United Nations* (New York: Columbia University Press, 1969).

PEACEKEEPING AND COLLECTIVE SECURITY

102   Abi-Saab, G., *The United Nations Operation in the Congo, 1960–1964* (Oxford: Oxford University Press, 1978).
103   Alden, C., 'The UN and the resolution of conflict in Mozambique', *Journal of Modern African Studies* 31(1) 1995, pp. 103–28.
104   Arend, A.C. and Beck, R.J., *International Law and the Use of Force: Beyond the UN Charter Paradigm* (London: Routledge, 1993).
105   Barnett, M., 'Partners in peace? The UN, regional organizations and peace-keeping', *Review of International Studies* 21(4) 1995, pp. 411–33.
106   Bell, C. (ed.), *The United Nations and Crisis Management: Six Studies* (Canberra: Australian National University, 1994).
107   Berdal, M., *Whither Peacekeeping?* (London: International Institute for Strategic Studies Adelphi Paper 81, 1993).

108 Berdal, M. and Leifer, M., 'Cambodia' in Mayall, J. (ed.), *The New Interventionism 1991–1994: United Nations Experience in Cambodia, Former Yugoslavia and Somalia* (Cambridge: Cambridge University Press, 1996), pp. 25–58.

109 Biermann, W., '"Old" UN peacekeeping and "new" conflicts: some ideas to reduce the troubles of post cold-war peace missions', *European Security* 4(1) 1995, pp. 39–55.

110 Bloomfield, L. *et al.*, *International Military Forces: The Question of Peacekeeping in an Armed and Disarming World* (Boston: Little, Brown, 1964).

111 Bowett, D., *United Nations Forces* (London: Stevens & Sons, 1964).

112 Boyd, J., *United Nations Peacekeeping Operations: A Military and Political Appraisal* (New York: Praeger, 1971).

113 Burns, A.L. and Heathcote, N., *Peacekeeping by UN Forces from Suez to the Congo* (London: Pall Mall, 1963).

114 Comay, M., *UN Peace-Keeping in the Arab-Israeli Conflict, 1948–1975* (Jerusalem: Hebrew University, 1976)

115 Cox, A.M., *Prospects for Peacekeeping* (Washington DC: Brookings Institute, 1967).

116 Diehl, P.F., *International Peacekeeping* (Baltimore: Johns Hopkins University Press, 1993).

117 Doyle, M.W., *UN Peacekeeping in Cambodia: UNTAC's Civil Mandate* (London: Rienner, 1995).

118 Durch, W. (ed.), *The Evolution of UN Peacekeeping: Case Studies and Comparative Analysis* (New York: St Martin's Press, 1993).

119 Economides, S. and Taylor, P., 'Former Yugoslavia' in Mayall, J. (ed.), *The New Interventionism 1991–1994: United Nations Experience in Cambodia, Former Yugoslavia and Somalia* (Cambridge: Cambridge University Press, 1996), pp. 59–93.

120 Fabian, L.L., *Soldiers without Enemies: Preparing the UN for Peacekeeping* (Washington DC: Brookings Institute, 1973).

121 Fetherston, A.B., *Towards a Theory of United Nations Peacekeeping* (London: Macmillan, 1994).

122 Fisas, V., *Blue Geopolitics: United Nations Reform and the Future of the Blue Helmets* (London: Pluto, 1995).

123 Goodrich, L.M. and Simmons, A., *The United Nations and the Maintenance of International Peace and Security* (Washington DC: Brookings Institute, 1955).

124 Gordenker, L., *The UN Secretary-General and the Maintenance of Peace* (New York: Columbia University Press, 1967).

125 Harbottle, M., *The Impartial Soldier: A Study of the UN Operation in Cyprus* (Oxford: Oxford University Press, 1970).

126 Harbottle, M., *The Blue Berets: The Story of United Nations Peacekeeping Forces* (London: Leo Cooper, 1971).

127   Harbottle, M. and Rikhye, I.J., *The Thin Blue Line: International Peacekeeping and its Future* (New Haven CT: Yale University Press, 1974).

128   Harrelson, M., *Fires all Around the Horizon: The UN's Uphill Battle to Preserve the Peace* (New York: Praeger, 1989).

129   Hill, S.M. and Malik, S.P., *Peacekeeping and the United Nations* (Aldershot: Dartmouth, 1996).

130   Howard, M., 'The historical development of the UN's role in international security', in Roberts, A. and Kingsbury, B. (eds), *United Nations, Divided World* (Oxford: Oxford University Press, 1993), pp. 63–80.

131   James, A., *The Politics of Peacekeeping* (London: Chatto & Windus, 1969).

132   James, A., 'The UN force in Cyprus', *International Affairs* 65(3) 1989, pp. 481–500.

133   James, A., *Peacekeeping in International Politics* (London: Macmillan, 1990).

134   Larus, J. (ed.), *From Collective Security to Preventive Diplomacy* (New York: Wiley, 1965).

135   Lash, J.P., *Dag Hammarskjöld: Custodian of the Brushfire Peace* (London: Cassell, 1962).

136   Lefever, E.W., *Crisis in the Congo: A United Nations Force in Action* (Washington DC: Brookings Institute, 1965).

137   Lefever, E.W., *Uncertain Mandate: The Politics of the UN Congo Operation* (Baltimore: Johns Hopkins University Press, 1967).

138   Lewis. I. and Mayall, J., 'Somalia' in Mayall, J. (ed.), *The New Interventionism 1991–1994: United Nations Experience in Cambodia, Former Yugoslavia and Somalia* (Cambridge: Cambridge University Press, 1996), pp. 94–124.

139   Mackinley, J., *The Peacekeepers* (London: Unwin Hyman, 1989).

140   Mayall, J., 'Introduction' in Mayall, J. (ed.), *The New Interventionism 1991–1994: United Nations Experience in Cambodia, Former Yugoslavia and Somalia* (Cambridge: Cambridge University Press, 1996), pp. 1–24.

141   Morphet, S., 'UN peacekeeping and election monitoring', in Roberts, A. and Kingsbury, B. (eds), *United Nations, Divided World* (Oxford: Oxford University Press, 1993), pp. 183–239.

142   Murphy, J.F., *The United Nations and the Control of International Violence* (Manchester: Manchester University Press, 1983).

143   Padelford, N., *The Financing of Future Peace and Security Operations under the United Nations* (Washington DC: Brookings Institute, 1962).

144   Parsons, A., *From Cold War to Hot Peace: UN Interventions 1975–1995* (Harmondsworth: Penguin, 1995).

145   Pugh, M., (ed.), *The UN, Peace and Force* (London: Frank Cass, 1997).

146 Ratner, S.R., *The New UN Peacekeeping: Building Peace in Lands of Conflict after the Cold War* (London: Macmillan, 1995).

147 Roberts, A., 'Communal conflict as a challenge to international organization: the case of the former Yugoslavia', *Review of International Studies* 21(4) 1995, pp. 389–410.

148 Roberts, A., 'The United Nations: variants of collective security' in Woods, N. (ed.), *Explaining International Relations since 1945* (Oxford: Oxford University Press, 1996), pp. 309–36.

149 Rosner, G., *The United Nations Emergency Force* (New York: Columbia University Press, 1963).

150 Russell, R.B., *United Nations Experience with Military Forces* (Washington DC: Brookings Institute, 1964).

151 Simmonds, R., *Legal Problems Arising from the United Nations Military Operations in the Congo* (The Hague: Nijhoff, 1968).

152 Skögmo, B., *UNIFIL: International Peacekeeping in Lebanon* (London: Rienner, 1989).

153 Stegenga, J.A., *The United Nations Force in Cyprus* (Columbus OH: Ohio State University Press, 1968).

154 Thakur, R., *International Peacekeeping in Lebanon* (Boulder CO: Westview, 1987).

155 Tharoor, S., 'United Nations peacekeeping in Europe', *Survival* 37(2) 1992, pp. 121–34.

156 Urquhart, B., 'Beyond the "sheriff's posse"', *Survival*, 32(3) 1990, pp. 196–205.

157 Urquhart, B., 'The UN and international security after the cold war', in Roberts, A. and Kingsbury, B. (eds), *United Nations, Divided World* (Oxford: Oxford University Press, 1993), pp. 81–103.

158 Verrier, A., *International Peacekeeping: United Nations Forces in a Troubled World* (Harmondsworth: Penguin, 1981).

159 Wainhouse, D.W., *et al.*, *International Peace Observation: A History and a Forecast* (Baltimore: Johns Hopkins University Press, 1966).

160 Wainhouse, D.W., *et al.*, *International Peacekeeping at the Crossroads* (Baltimore: Johns Hopkins University Press, 1973).

161 Weiss, T.G., *Collective Security in a Changing World* (London: Rienner, 1994).

162 White, N.D., *The United Nations and the Maintenance of International Peace and Security* (Manchester: Manchester University Press, 1990).

163 Zacher, M.W., *International Conflict and Collective Security 1946–77: The United Nations, the Organization of American States, the Organization of African Unity and the Arab League* (New York: Praeger, 1979).

INDEX